I HAVE PUT MY HOPE IN YOUR WORD!
— Psalm 119:47

Amanda Torres

This Belongs to:
Amanda Torres

QUIET TIME//

ONE-YEAR DAILY
DEVOTIONAL FOR
STUDENTS

QUIET TIME FOR STUDENTS

Word of Life Fellowship, Inc.
Don Lough – Executive Director
Jack Wyrtzen & Harry Bollback – Founders
Ric Garland – VP of Local Church Ministries

USA
P.O. Box 600
Schroon Lake, NY 12870
talk@wol.org
1-888-932-5827

Canada
RR#8/Owen Sound
ON, Canada N4K 5W4
LCM@wol.ca
1-800-461-3503

Web Address: www.wol.org

PUBLISHER'S ACKNOWLEDGEMENTS

Writers and Contributors:

Bobby Barton	Acts (Chapters 1-12), Deuteronomy
Matt Boutilier	Psalms
Cory Fehr	Jeremiah, 1, 2, 3, John, 1 Timothy
Andy Grenier	Galatians, Acts (Chapters 13-end)
Dave Huizing	Daniel
Joe and Gloria Phillips	Proverbs, Job, Habakkuk, Zephaniah, Colossians, Joel
Matt Walls	1 Thessalonians, 2 Peter, Jude

Editor: Dale Flynn
Curriculum Manager: Don Reichard
Cover and page design: Visional Design, David Choate

ISBN: 978-1-935475-23-1
Printed in the United States of America

HELPFUL HINTS FOR A DAILY QUIET TIME

The purpose of this Quiet Time is to meet the needs of spiritual growth in the life of the Christian in such a way that they learn the art of conducting their own personal investigation into the Bible. Consider the following helpful hints:

1 Give priority in choosing your quiet time. This will vary with each individual in accordance with his own circumstances. The time you choose must:
- have top priority over everything else
- be the quietest time possible.
- be a convenient time of the day or night.
- be consistently observed each day.

2 Give attention to the procedure suggested for you to follow. Include the following items.
- Read God's Word.
- Mark your Bible as you read. Here are some suggestions that might be helpful:
  a. After you read the passage put an exclamation mark next to the verses you completely understand.
  b. Put a question mark next to verses you do not understand.
  c. Put an arrow pointing upward next to encouraging verses.
  d. Put an arrow pointing downward next to verses which challenge you spiritually.
  e. Put a star next to verses containing important truths or major points.
- Meditate on what you have read (In one sentence, write the main thought). Here are some suggestions as guidelines for meditating on God's Word:
  a. Look at the selected passage from God's point of view.
  b. Though we encourage quiet time in the morning, some people arrange to have their quiet time at the end of their day. God emphasizes that we need to go to sleep

meditating on His Word. "My soul shall be satisfied and my mouth shall praise thee with joyful lips: when I remember thee upon my bed, and meditating on thee in the night watches" (Psalm 63:5,6).

c. Deuteronomy 6:7 lists routine things you do each day during which you should concentrate on the portion of Scripture for that day:

— when you sit in your house (meals and relaxation)
— when you walk in the way (to and from school or work)
— when you lie down (before going to sleep at night)
— when you rise up (getting ready for the day)

Apply some truth to your life. (Use first person pronouns I, me, my, mine). If you have difficulty in finding an application for your life, think of yourself as a Bible SPECTator and ask yourself the following questions.

S – is there any SIN for me to forsake?

P – is there any PROMISE for me to claim?

E – is there any EXAMPLE for me to follow?

C – is there any COMMAND for me to obey?

T – is there anything to be THANKFUL for today?

Pray for specific things (Use the prayer sheets found in the My Prayer Journal section).

3   Be sure to fill out your quiet time sheets. This will really help you remember the things the Lord brings to your mind.

4   Purpose to share with someone else each day something you gained from your quiet time. This can be a real blessing for them as well as for you.

HELPFUL HINTS FOR A
DAILY QUIET TIME

The Quiet Time for Students will help you have a special time each day with the Lord. The daily passages are organized so that you cover every book of the Bible in six years. All Word of Life quiet times use the same daily passage for all ages, so families, small groups, or even entire churches can encourage each other from the Word of God.

The following instructions walk you through the steps for using the Quiet Time.

> First read the weekly overview to learn what the focus is for the coming week.

WEEK 8

Have you ever wondered what to look for in a friend, what gives a person true value, or even how to be prosperous in life? This week in Proverbs we'll look at these questions and find answers to other everyday questions. We'll even find out how to tell the difference between wise and foolish people.

PRAYER FOCUS FOR THIS WEEK

> Use this area to write prayer requests and reminders for the week.

THE QUESTION: What is the writer saying?
THE ANSWER: How can I apply this to my life?

SUNDAY • Proverbs 26:1-16

Q
A

> Next, listen to the Lord as you read the daily passage.

DIGGING DEEPER .... of Proverbs and said, "Duh, *that's* obvious!"? Other tim................................. to get at the meaning. That's because a proverb is a ge................................ em to contradict each other. Solomon says in verse 4................................ ld not answer a fool because he doesn't really care .... ower ourselves to his level. Other times we should answer so he won't go around thinking highly of himself and further harming others. How do you know the difference? Becoming wise and reading the book of Proverbs is a great start. At the end of our passage today we see some reminders of the crazy excuses lazy people use.
Some of the hardest parts of being wise involve knowing how to deal with people. How can you ask God for help in this area today?

> Now share your thoughts as you answer the two questions.

5

MONDAY • Proverbs 26:17-28

DIGGING DEEPER Have you ever tried to break up a fight only to have both people turn on you? How about having a practical joke backfire? Solomon gives a severe warning against deceiving people and then telling them you were just kidding. The rest of the passage today deals with controlling the tongue. First, we are told not to pass on rumors—this reveals our heart problem of not caring about the people we talk about. On the other hand, sometimes we misuse our tongue and give flattering remarks to people and really don't mean it. Solomon warns us that this is not only bad because it is untrue but also because it will harm us in the long run.

sage looked at some things we probably do all the time without omon says these actions can really hurt people, though. Do any out to you as something you need to change?

> *Take time to read the Digging Deeper commentary for additional insights on the text.*

TUESDAY • Proverbs 27:1-9

DIGGING DEEPER What are your friends like? What kind of friend are you? Today's passage deals with these questions. In verses 1-2, we see someone who is humble. Those people don't boast about themse... they are before God. When you know who you ar... others. Next, Solomon says a friend is open to c... Throughout Proverbs we see that a fool rejects... it. A good friend does the loving thing to help us overcome our faults... the glory of God.

> *Consider these questions as you begin your prayer time.*

Humility and being a good friend start with us understanding our place before God. Ask God to help you learn about Him today, and to show you specific situations where you can be a good friend to others.

> *Use the weekly and daily prayer pages in the front of the Quiet Time to organize your prayer time as God leads you.*

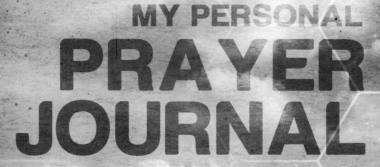

MY PERSONAL
PRAYER
JOURNAL

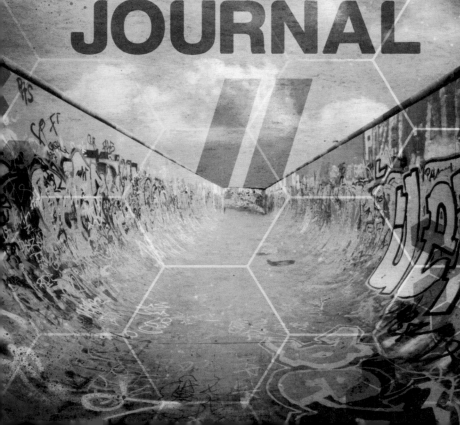

SUNDAY

FAMILY

CHRISTIAN FRIENDS

UNSAVED FRIENDS

MISSIONARIES

MONDAY

FAMILY

CHRISTIAN FRIENDS

UNSAVED FRIENDS

MISSIONARIES

TUESDAY

FAMILY

CHRISTIAN FRIENDS

UNSAVED FRIENDS

MISSIONARIES

WEDNESDAY

FAMILY

CHRISTIAN FRIENDS

UNSAVED FRIENDS

MISSIONARIES

THURSDAY

FAMILY

CHRISTIAN FRIENDS

UNSAVED FRIENDS

MISSIONARIES

FRIDAY

FAMILY

CHRISTIAN FRIENDS

UNSAVED FRIENDS

MISSIONARIES

SATURDAY

FAMILY

CHRISTIAN FRIENDS

UNSAVED FRIENDS

MISSIONARIES

PRAISE LIST

Serina + Scout
        (they lost 11 month child)

Mr. Rodney

9/11/11
9/11/01 Survivors + their families
Pastor Rodney + family
Church + Building Funds

PRAISE LIST

DATE/ANSWER

PRAISE LIST

DATE/ANSWER

PRAISE LIST

DATE/ANSWER

PRAISE LIST

DATE/ANSWER

Some people just can't get enough! That is why we have several dimensions in the Word of Life Quiet Time. Along with the daily reading, content and application questions for each day, two reading programs are given to help you understand the Bible better. Choose one or both.

Reading Through the New Testament Four Times In One Year

Turn the page and discover a schedule that takes you through the New Testament four times in one year. This is a great method to help you see the correlation of the Gospels and other New Testament books.

Reading Through the Whole Bible In One Year

Turn another page and find a program of several pages that will guide you through a chronological reading of the entire Bible. Follow this schedule and you will move from Genesis through Revelation in one year.

The Choice is Up to You

Whether you have a short quiet time, a quiet time with more scripture reading or one with a mini-Bible study each day, we trust your time with God will draw you closer to Him in every area of your life.

READ THROUGH THE NEW TESTAMENT
FOUR TIMES IN ONE YEAR

Weeks 1-13

- ☐ Matthew 1-3
- ☐ Matthew 4-6
- ☐ Matthew 7-9
- ☐ Matt. 10-12
- ☐ Matt. 13-15
- ☐ Matt. 16-18
- ☐ Matt. 19-21
- ☐ Matt. 22-24
- ☐ Matt. 25-26
- ☐ Matt. 27-28
- ☐ Mark 1-3
- ☐ Mark 4-5
- ☐ Mark 6-8
- ☐ Mark 9-11
- ☐ Mark 12-14
- ☐ Mark 15-16
- ☐ Luke 1-2
- ☐ Luke 3-5
- ☐ Luke 6-7
- ☐ Luke 8-9
- ☐ Luke 10-11
- ☐ Luke 12-14
- ☐ Luke 15-17
- ☐ Luke 18-20
- ☐ Luke 21-22
- ☐ Luke 23-24
- ☐ John 1-3
- ☐ John 4-5
- ☐ John 6-7
- ☐ John 8-10
- ☐ John 11-12
- ☐ John 13-15
- ☐ John 16-18
- ☐ John 19-21
- ☐ Acts 1-3
- ☐ Acts 4-6
- ☐ Acts 7-8
- ☐ Acts 9-11
- ☐ Acts 12-15
- ☐ Acts 16-18
- ☐ Acts 19-21
- ☐ Acts 22-24
- ☐ Acts 25-26
- ☐ Acts 27-28
- ☐ Romans 1-3

- ☐ Romans 4-6
- ☐ Romans 7-9
- ☐ Romans 10-12
- ☐ Romans 13-16
- ☐ 1 Cor. 1-4
- ☐ 1 Cor. 5-9
- ☐ 1 Cor. 10-12
- ☐ 1 Cor. 13-16
- ☐ 2 Cor. 1-4
- ☐ 2 Cor. 5-8
- ☐ 2 Cor. 9-13
- ☐ Galatians 1-3
- ☐ Galatians 4-6
- ☐ Ephesians 1-3
- ☐ Ephesians 4-6
- ☐ Philippians 1-4
- ☐ Colossians 1-4
- ☐ 1 Thes. 1-3
- ☐ 1 Thes. 4-5
- ☐ 2 Thes. 1-3
- ☐ 1 Timothy 1-3
- ☐ 1 Timothy 4-6
- ☐ 2 Timothy 1-4
- ☐ Titus 1-3
- ☐ Philemon
- ☐ Hebrews 1
- ☐ Hebrews 2-4
- ☐ Hebrews 5-7
- ☐ Hebrews 8-10
- ☐ Hebrews 11-13
- ☐ James 1-3
- ☐ James 4-5
- ☐ 1 Peter 1-3
- ☐ 1 Peter 4-5
- ☐ 2 Peter 1-3
- ☐ 1 John 1-3
- ☐ 1 John 4-5
- ☐ 2 Jn, 3 Jn, Jude
- ☐ Revelation 1-3
- ☐ Revelation 4-6
- ☐ Revelation 7-9
- ☐ Rev. 10-12
- ☐ Rev. 13-15
- ☐ Rev. 16-18
- ☐ Rev. 19-22

Weeks 14-26

- ☐ Matthew 1-3
- ☐ Matthew 4-6
- ☐ Matthew 7-9
- ☐ Matt. 10-12
- ☐ Matt. 13-15
- ☐ Matt. 16-18
- ☐ Matt. 19-21
- ☐ Matt. 22-24
- ☐ Matt. 25-26
- ☐ Matt. 27-28
- ☐ Mark 1-3
- ☐ Mark 4-5
- ☐ Mark 6-8
- ☐ Mark 9-11
- ☐ Mark 12-14
- ☐ Mark 15-16
- ☐ Luke 1-2
- ☐ Luke 3-5
- ☐ Luke 6-7
- ☐ Luke 8-9
- ☐ Luke 10-11
- ☐ Luke 12-14
- ☐ Luke 15-17
- ☐ Luke 18-20
- ☐ Luke 21-22
- ☐ Luke 23-24
- ☐ John 1-3
- ☐ John 4-5
- ☐ John 6-7
- ☐ John 8-10
- ☐ John 11-12
- ☐ John 13-15
- ☐ John 16-18
- ☐ John 19-21
- ☐ Acts 1-3
- ☐ Acts 4-6
- ☐ Acts 7-8
- ☐ Acts 9-11
- ☐ Acts 12-15
- ☐ Acts 16-18
- ☐ Acts 19-21
- ☐ Acts 22-24
- ☐ Acts 25-26
- ☐ Acts 27-28
- ☐ Romans 1-3

- ☐ Romans 4-6
- ☐ Romans 7-9
- ☐ Romans 10-12
- ☐ Romans 13-16
- ☐ 1 Cor. 1-4
- ☐ 1 Cor. 5-9
- ☐ 1 Cor. 10-12
- ☐ 1 Cor. 13-16
- ☐ 2 Cor. 1-4
- ☐ 2 Cor. 5-8
- ☐ 2 Cor. 9-13
- ☐ Galatians 1-3
- ☐ Galatians 4-6
- ☐ Ephesians 1-3
- ☐ Ephesians 4-6
- ☐ Philippians 1-4
- ☐ Colossians 1-4
- ☐ 1 Thes. 1-3
- ☐ 1 Thes. 4-5
- ☐ 2 Thes. 1-3
- ☐ 1 Timothy 1-3
- ☐ 1 Timothy 4-6
- ☐ 2 Timothy 1-4
- ☐ Titus 1-3
- ☐ Philemon
- ☐ Hebrews 1
- ☐ Hebrews 2-4
- ☐ Hebrews 5-7
- ☐ Hebrews 8-10
- ☐ Hebrews 11-13
- ☐ James 1-3
- ☐ James 4-5
- ☐ 1 Peter 1-3
- ☐ 1 Peter 4-5
- ☐ 2 Peter 1-3
- ☐ 1 John 1-3
- ☐ 1 John 4-5
- ☐ 2 Jn, 3 Jn, Jude
- ☐ Revelation 1-3
- ☐ Revelation 4-6
- ☐ Revelation 7-9
- ☐ Rev. 10-12
- ☐ Rev. 13-15
- ☐ Rev. 16-18
- ☐ Rev. 19-22

READ THROUGH THE NEW TESTAMENT
FOUR TIMES IN ONE YEAR

Weeks 27-39

- ☐ Matthew 1-3
- ☐ Matthew 4-6
- ☐ Matthew 7-9
- ☐ Matt. 10-12
- ☐ Matt. 13-15
- ☐ Matt. 16-18
- ☐ Matt. 19-21
- ☐ Matt. 22-24
- ☐ Matt. 25-26
- ☐ Matt. 27-28
- ☐ Mark 1-3
- ☐ Mark 4-5
- ☐ Mark 6-8
- ☐ Mark 9-11
- ☐ Mark 12-14
- ☐ Mark 15-16
- ☐ Luke 1-2
- ☐ Luke 3-5
- ☐ Luke 6-7
- ☐ Luke 8-9
- ☐ Luke 10-11
- ☐ Luke 12-14
- ☐ Luke 15-17
- ☐ Luke 18-20
- ☐ Luke 21-22
- ☐ Luke 23-24
- ☐ John 1-3
- ☐ John 4-5
- ☐ John 6-7
- ☐ John 8-10
- ☐ John 11-12
- ☐ John 13-15
- ☐ John 16-18
- ☐ John 19-21
- ☐ Acts 1-3
- ☐ Acts 4-6
- ☐ Acts 7-8
- ☐ Acts 9-11
- ☐ Acts 12-15
- ☐ Acts 16-18
- ☐ Acts 19-21
- ☐ Acts 22-24
- ☐ Acts 25-26
- ☐ Acts 27-28
- ☐ Romans 1-3

- ☐ Romans 4-6
- ☐ Romans 7-9
- ☐ Romans 10-12
- ☐ Romans 13-16
- ☐ 1 Cor. 1-4
- ☐ 1 Cor. 5-9
- ☐ 1 Cor. 10-12
- ☐ 1 Cor. 13-16
- ☐ 2 Cor. 1-4
- ☐ 2 Cor. 5-8
- ☐ 2 Cor. 9-13
- ☐ Galatians 1-3
- ☐ Galatians 4-6
- ☐ Ephesians 1-3
- ☐ Ephesians 4-6
- ☐ Phil. 1-4
- ☐ Colossians 1-4
- ☐ 1 Thes. 1-3
- ☐ 1 Thes. 4-5
- ☐ 2 Thes. 1-3
- ☐ 1 Timothy 1-3
- ☐ 1 Timothy 4-6
- ☐ 2 Timothy 1-4
- ☐ Titus 1-3
- ☐ Philemon
- ☐ Hebrews 1
- ☐ Hebrews 2-4
- ☐ Hebrews 5-7
- ☐ Hebrews 8-10
- ☐ Hebrews 11-13
- ☐ James 1-3
- ☐ James 4-5
- ☐ 1 Peter 1-3
- ☐ 1 Peter 4-5
- ☐ 2 Peter 1-3
- ☐ 1 John 1-3
- ☐ 1 John 4-5
- ☐ 2 Jn, 3 Jn, Jude
- ☐ Revelation 1-3
- ☐ Revelation 4-6
- ☐ Revelation 7-9
- ☐ Rev. 10-12
- ☐ Rev. 13-15
- ☐ Rev. 16-18
- ☐ Rev. 19-22

Weeks 40-52

- ☐ Matthew 1-3
- ☐ Matthew 4-6
- ☐ Matthew 7-9
- ☐ Matt. 10-12
- ☐ Matt. 13-15
- ☐ Matt. 16-18
- ☐ Matt. 19-21
- ☐ Matt. 22-24
- ☐ Matt. 25-26
- ☐ Matt. 27-28
- ☐ Mark 1-3
- ☐ Mark 4-5
- ☐ Mark 6-8
- ☐ Mark 9-11
- ☐ Mark 12-14
- ☐ Mark 15-16
- ☐ Luke 1-2
- ☐ Luke 3-5
- ☐ Luke 6-7
- ☐ Luke 8-9
- ☐ Luke 10-11
- ☐ Luke 12-14
- ☐ Luke 15-17
- ☐ Luke 18-20
- ☐ Luke 21-22
- ☐ Luke 23-24
- ☐ John 1-3
- ☐ John 4-5
- ☐ John 6-7
- ☐ John 8-10
- ☐ John 11-12
- ☐ John 13-15
- ☐ John 16-18
- ☐ John 19-21
- ☐ Acts 1-3
- ☐ Acts 4-6
- ☐ Acts 7-8
- ☐ Acts 9-11
- ☐ Acts 12-15
- ☐ Acts 16-18
- ☐ Acts 19-21
- ☐ Acts 22-24
- ☐ Acts 25-26
- ☐ Acts 27-28
- ☐ Romans 1-3

- ☐ Romans 4-6
- ☐ Romans 7-9
- ☐ Romans 10-12
- ☐ Romans 13-16
- ☐ 1 Cor. 1-4
- ☐ 1 Cor. 5-9
- ☐ 1 Cor. 10-12
- ☐ 1 Cor. 13-16
- ☐ 2 Cor. 1-4
- ☐ 2 Cor. 5-8
- ☐ 2 Cor. 9-13
- ☐ Galatians 1-3
- ☐ Galatians 4-6
- ☐ Ephesians 1-3
- ☐ Ephesians 4-6
- ☐ Phil. 1-4
- ☐ Colossians 1-4
- ☐ 1 Thes. 1-3
- ☐ 1 Thes. 4-5
- ☐ 2 Thes. 1-3
- ☐ 1 Timothy 1-3
- ☐ 1 Timothy 4-6
- ☐ 2 Timothy 1-4
- ☐ Titus 1-3
- ☐ Philemon
- ☐ Hebrews 1
- ☐ Hebrews 2-4
- ☐ Hebrews 5-7
- ☐ Hebrews 8-10
- ☐ Hebrews 11-13
- ☐ James 1-3
- ☐ James 4-5
- ☐ 1 Peter 1-3
- ☐ 1 Peter 4-5
- ☐ 2 Peter 1-3
- ☐ 1 John 1-3
- ☐ 1 John 4-5
- ☐ 2 Jn, 3 Jn, Jude
- ☐ Revelation 1-3
- ☐ Revelation 4-6
- ☐ Revelation 7-9
- ☐ Rev. 10-12
- ☐ Rev. 13-15
- ☐ Rev. 16-18
- ☐ Rev. 19-22

BIBLE READING SCHEDULE

Read through the Bible in one year! As you complete each daily reading, simply place a check in the appropriate box.

☐ 1 Genesis 1-3	☐ 53 Leviticus 18-20
☐ 2 Genesis 4:1-6:8	☐ 54 Leviticus 21-23
☐ 3 Genesis 6:9-9:29	☐ 55 Leviticus 24-25
☐ 4 Genesis 10-11	☐ 56 Leviticus 26-27
☐ 5 Genesis 12-14	☐ 57 Numbers 1-2
☐ 6 Genesis 15-17	☐ 58 Numbers 3-4
☐ 7 Genesis 18-19	☐ 59 Numbers 5-6
☐ 8 Genesis 20-22	☐ 60 Numbers 7
☐ 9 Genesis 23-24	☐ 61 Numbers 8-10
☐ 10 Genesis 25-26	☐ 62 Numbers 11-13
☐ 11 Genesis 27-28	☐ 63 Numbers 14-15
☐ 12 Genesis 29-30	☐ 64 Numbers 16-18
☐ 13 Genesis 31-32	☐ 65 Numbers 19-21
☐ 14 Genesis 33-35	☐ 66 Numbers 22-24
☐ 15 Genesis 36-37	☐ 67 Numbers 25-26
☐ 16 Genesis 38-40	☐ 68 Numbers 27-29
☐ 17 Genesis 41-42	☐ 69 Numbers 30-31
☐ 18 Genesis 43-45	☐ 70 Numbers 32-33
☐ 19 Genesis 46-47	☐ 71 Numbers 34-36
☐ 20 Genesis 48-50	☐ 72 Deuteronomy 1-2
☐ 21 Job 1-3	☐ 73 Deuteronomy 3-4
☐ 22 Job 4-7	☐ 74 Deuteronomy 5-7
☐ 23 Job 8-11	☐ 75 Deuteronomy 8-10
☐ 24 Job 12-15	☐ 76 Deuteronomy 11-13
☐ 25 Job 16-19	☐ 77 Deuteronomy 14-17
☐ 26 Job 20-22	☐ 78 Deuteronomy 18-21
☐ 27 Job 23-28	☐ 79 Deuteronomy 22-25
☐ 28 Job 29-31	☐ 80 Deuteronomy 26-28
☐ 29 Job 32-34	☐ 81 Deuteronomy 29:1-31:29
☐ 30 Job 35-37	☐ 82 Deuteronomy 31:30-34:12
☐ 31 Job 38-42	☐ 83 Joshua 1-4
☐ 32 Exodus 1-4	☐ 84 Joshua 5-8
☐ 33 Exodus 5-8	☐ 85 Joshua 9-11
☐ 34 Exodus 9-11	☐ 86 Joshua 12-14
☐ 35 Exodus 12-13	☐ 87 Joshua 15-17
☐ 36 Exodus 14-15	☐ 88 Joshua 18-19
☐ 37 Exodus 16-18	☐ 89 Joshua 20-22
☐ 38 Exodus 19-21	☐ 90 Joshua 23 - Judges 1
☐ 39 Exodus 22-24	☐ 91 Judges 2-5
☐ 40 Exodus 25-27	☐ 92 Judges 6-8
☐ 41 Exodus 28-29	☐ 93 Judges 9
☐ 42 Exodus 30-31	☐ 94 Judges 10-12
☐ 43 Exodus 32-34	☐ 95 Judges 13-16
☐ 44 Exodus 35-36	☐ 96 Judges 17-19
☐ 45 Exodus 37-38	☐ 97 Judges 20-21
☐ 46 Exodus 39-40	☐ 98 Ruth
☐ 47 Leviticus 1:1-5:13	☐ 99 1 Samuel 1-3
☐ 48 Leviticus 5:14-7:38	☐ 100 1 Samuel 4-7
☐ 49 Leviticus 8-10	☐ 101 1 Samuel 8-10
☐ 50 Leviticus 11-12	☐ 102 1 Samuel 11-13
☐ 51 Leviticus 13-14	☐ 103 1 Samuel 14-15
☐ 52 Leviticus 15-17	☐ 104 1 Samuel 16-17

BIBLE READING SCHEDULE

Day 105 - 199

- ☐ 105 1 Samuel 18-19; Psalm 59
- ☐ 106 1 Samuel 20-21; Psalm 56; 34
- ☐ 107 1 Samuel 22-23; 1 Chronicles 12:8-18; Psalm 52; 54; 63; 142
- ☐ 108 1 Samuel 24; Psalm 57; 1 Samuel 25
- ☐ 109 1 Samuel 26-29; 1 Chronicles 12:1-7, 19-22
- ☐ 110 1 Samuel 30-31; 1 Chronicles 10; 2 Samuel 1
- ☐ 111 2 Samuel 2-4
- ☐ 112 2 Samuel 5:1-6:11; 1 Chronicles 11:1-9; 13:1-14:17
- ☐ 113 2 Samuel 22; Psalm 18
- ☐ 114 1 Chronicles 15-16; 2 Samuel 6:12-23; Psalm 96
- ☐ 115 Psalm 105; 2 Samuel 7; 1 Chronicles 17
- ☐ 116 2 Samuel 8-10; 1 Chronicles 18-19; Psalm 60
- ☐ 117 2 Samuel 11-12; 1 Chronicles 20:1-3; Psalm 51
- ☐ 118 2 Samuel 13-14
- ☐ 119 2 Samuel 15-17
- ☐ 120 Psalm 3; 2 Samuel 18-19
- ☐ 121 2 Samuel 20-21; 23:8-23; 1 Chronicles 20:4-8; 11:10-25
- ☐ 122 2 Samuel 23:24-24:25;
- ☐ 123 1 Chronicles 11:26-47; 21:1-30, 1 Chronicles 22-24
- ☐ 124 Psalm 30; 1 Chronicles 25-26
- ☐ 125 1 Chronicles 27-29
- ☐ 126 Psalms 5-7; 10; 11; 13; 17
- ☐ 127 Psalms 23; 26; 28; 31; 35
- ☐ 128 Psalms 41; 43; 46; 55; 61; 62; 64
- ☐ 129 Psalms 69-71; 77
- ☐ 130 Psalms 83; 86; 88; 91; 95
- ☐ 131 Psalms 108-9; 120-21; 140; 143-44
- ☐ 132 Psalms 1; 14-15; 36-37; 39
- ☐ 133 Psalms 40; 49-50; 73
- ☐ 134 Psalms 76; 82; 84; 90; 92; 112; 115
- ☐ 135 Psalms 8-9; 16; 19; 21; 24; 29
- ☐ 136 Psalms 33; 65-68
- ☐ 137 Psalms 75; 93-94; 97-100
- ☐ 138 Psalms 103-4; 113-14; 117
- ☐ 139 Psalm 119:1-88
- ☐ 140 Psalm 119:89-176
- ☐ 141 Psalms 122; 124; 133-36
- ☐ 142 Psalms 138-39; 145; 148; 150
- ☐ 143 Psalms 4; 12; 20; 25; 32; 38
- ☐ 144 Psalms 42; 53; 58; 81; 101; 111; 130-31; 141; 146
- ☐ 145 Psalms 2; 22; 27
- ☐ 146 Psalms 45; 47-48; 87; 110
- ☐ 147 1 Kings 1:1-2:12; 2 Samuel 23:1-7
- ☐ 148 1 Kings 2:13-3:28; 2 Chronicles 1:1-13
- ☐ 149 1 Kings 5-6; 2 Chronicles 2-3
- ☐ 150 1 Kings 7; 2 Chronicles 4
- ☐ 151 1 Kings 8; 2 Chronicles 5:1-7:10
- ☐ 152 1 Kings 9:1-10:13; 2 Chronicles 7:11-9:12
- ☐ 153 1 Kings 4; 10:14-29; 2 Chronicles 1:14-17; 9:13-28; Psalm 72
- ☐ 154 Proverbs 1-3
- ☐ 155 Proverbs 4-6
- ☐ 156 Proverbs 7-9
- ☐ 157 Proverbs 10-12
- ☐ 158 Proverbs 13-15
- ☐ 159 Proverbs 16-18
- ☐ 160 Proverbs 19-21
- ☐ 161 Proverbs 22-24
- ☐ 162 Proverbs 25-27
- ☐ 163 Proverbs 28-29
- ☐ 164 Proverbs 30-31; Psalm 127
- ☐ 165 Song of Solomon
- ☐ 166 1 Kings 11:1-40; Ecclesiastes 1-2
- ☐ 167 Ecclesiastes 3-7
- ☐ 168 Ecclesiastes 8-12; 1 Kings 11:41-43; 2 Chronicles 9:29-31
- ☐ 169 1 Kings 12; 2 Chronicles 10:1-11:17
- ☐ 170 1 Kings 13-14; 2 Chronicles 11:18-12:16
- ☐ 171 1 Kings 15:1-24; 2 Chronicles 13-16
- ☐ 172 1 Kings 15:25-16:34; 2 Chronicles 17; 1 Kings 17
- ☐ 173 1 Kings 18-19
- ☐ 174 1 Kings 20-21
- ☐ 175 1 Kings 22:1-40; 2 Chronicles 18
- ☐ 176 1 Kings 22:41-53; 2 Kings 1; 2 Chronicles 19:1-21:3
- ☐ 177 2 Kings 2-4
- ☐ 178 2 Kings 5-7
- ☐ 179 2 Kings 8-9; 2 Chronicles 21:4-22:9
- ☐ 180 2 Kings 10-11; 2 Chronicles 22:10-23:21
- ☐ 181 Joel
- ☐ 182 2 Kings 12-13; 2 Chronicles 24
- ☐ 183 2 Kings 14; 2 Chronicles 25; Jonah
- ☐ 184 Hosea 1-7
- ☐ 185 Hosea 8-14
- ☐ 186 2 Kings 15:1-7; 2 Chronicles 26; Amos 1-4
- ☐ 187 Amos 5-9; 2 Kings 15:8-18
- ☐ 188 Isaiah 1-4
- ☐ 189 2 Kings 15:19-38; 2 Chronicles 27; Isaiah 5-6
- ☐ 190 Micah
- ☐ 191 2 Kings 16; 2 Chronicles 28; Isaiah 7-8
- ☐ 192 Isaiah 9-12
- ☐ 193 Isaiah 13-16
- ☐ 194 Isaiah 17-22
- ☐ 195 Isaiah 23-27
- ☐ 196 Isaiah 28-30
- ☐ 197 Isaiah 31-35
- ☐ 198 2 Kings 18:1-8; 2 Chronicles 29-31
- ☐ 199 2 Kings 17; 18:9-37; 2 Chronicles 32:1-19; Isaiah 36

BIBLE READING SCHEDULE
Day 200 - 288

- [ ] 200 2 Kings 19; 2 Chronicles 32:20-23; Isaiah 37
- [ ] 201 2 Kings 20; 2 Chronicles 32:24-33; Isaiah 38-39
- [ ] 202 2 Kings 21:1-18; 2 Chronicles 33:1-20; Isaiah 40
- [ ] 203 Isaiah 41-43
- [ ] 204 Isaiah 44-47
- [ ] 205 Isaiah 48-51
- [ ] 206 Isaiah 52-57
- [ ] 207 Isaiah 58-62
- [ ] 208 Isaiah 63-66
- [ ] 209 2 Kings 21:19-26; 2 Chronicles 33:21-34:7; Zephaniah
- [ ] 210 Jeremiah 1-3
- [ ] 211 Jeremiah 4-6
- [ ] 212 Jeremiah 7-9
- [ ] 213 Jeremiah 10-13
- [ ] 214 Jeremiah 14-16
- [ ] 215 Jeremiah 17-20
- [ ] 216 2 Kings 22:1-23:28; 2 Chronicles 34:8-35:19
- [ ] 217 Nahum; 2 Kings 23:29-37;
- [ ] 2 Chronicles 35:20-36:5; Jeremiah 22:10-17
- [ ] 218 Jeremiah 26; Habakkuk
- [ ] 219 Jeremiah 46-47; 2 Kings 24:1-4, 7; 2 Chronicles 36:6-7; Jeremiah 25, 35
- [ ] 220 Jeremiah 36, 45, 48
- [ ] 221 Jeremiah 49:1-33; Daniel 1-2
- [ ] 222 Jeremiah 22:18-30; 2 Kings 24:5-20; 2 Chronicles 36:8-12; Jeremiah 37:1-2; 52:1-3; 24; 29
- [ ] 223 Jeremiah 27-28, 23
- [ ] 224 Jeremiah 50-51
- [ ] 225 Jeremiah 49:34-39; 34:1-22; Ezekiel 1-3
- [ ] 226 Ezekiel 4-7
- [ ] 227 Ezekiel 8-11
- [ ] 228 Ezekiel 12-14
- [ ] 229 Ezekiel 15-17
- [ ] 230 Ezekiel 18-20
- [ ] 231 Ezekiel 21-23
- [ ] 232 2 Kings 25:1; 2 Chronicles 36:13-16; Jeremiah 39:1; 52:4; Ezekiel 24; Jeremiah 21:1-22:9; 32:1-44
- [ ] 233 Jeremiah 30-31, 33
- [ ] 234 Ezekiel 25; 29:1-16; 30; 31
- [ ] 235 Ezekiel 26-28
- [ ] 236 Jeremiah 37:3-39:10; 52:5-30; 2 Kings 25:2-21; 2 Chronicles 36:17-21
- [ ] 237 2 Kings 25:22; Jeremiah 39:11-40:6; Lamentations 1-3
- [ ] 238 Lamentations 4-5; Obadiah
- [ ] 239 Jeremiah 40:7-44:30; 2 Kings 25:23-26
- [ ] 240 Ezekiel 33:21-36:38
- [ ] 241 Ezekiel 37-39
- [ ] 242 Ezekiel 32:1-33:20; Daniel 3
- [ ] 243 Ezekiel 40-42
- [ ] 244 Ezekiel 43-45
- [ ] 245 Ezekiel 46-48
- [ ] 246 Ezekiel 29:17-21; Daniel 4; Jeremiah 52:31-34; 2 Kings 25:27-30; Psalm 44
- [ ] 247 Psalms 74; 79-80; 89
- [ ] 248 Psalms 85; 102; 106; 123; 137
- [ ] 249 Daniel 7-8; 5
- [ ] 250 Daniel 9; 6
- [ ] 251 2 Chronicles 36:22-23; Ezra 1:1-4:5
- [ ] 252 Daniel 10-12
- [ ] 253 Ezra 4:6-6:13; Haggai
- [ ] 254 Zechariah 1-6
- [ ] 255 Zechariah 7-8; Ezra 6:14-22; Psalm 78
- [ ] 256 Psalms 107; 116; 118
- [ ] 257 Psalms 125-26; 128-29; 132; 147; 149
- [ ] 258 Zechariah 9-14
- [ ] 259 Esther 1-4
- [ ] 260 Esther 5-10
- [ ] 261 Ezra 7-8
- [ ] 262 Ezra 9-10
- [ ] 263 Nehemiah 1-5
- [ ] 264 Nehemiah 6-7
- [ ] 265 Nehemiah 8-10
- [ ] 266 Nehemiah 11-13
- [ ] 267 Malachi
- [ ] 268 1 Chronicles 1-2
- [ ] 269 1 Chronicles 3-5
- [ ] 270 1 Chronicles 6
- [ ] 271 1 Chronicles 7:1-8:27
- [ ] 272 1 Chronicles 8:28-9:44
- [ ] 273 John 1:1-18; Mark 1:1; Luke 1:1-4; 3:23-38; Matthew 1:1-17
- [ ] 274 Luke 1:5-80
- [ ] 275 Matthew 1:18-2:23; Luke 2
- [ ] 276 Matthew 3:1-4:11; Mark 1:2-13; Luke 3:1-23; 4:1-13; John 1:19-34
- [ ] 277 John 1:35-3:36
- [ ] 278 John 4; Matthew 4:12-17; Mark 1:14-15; Luke 4:14-30
- [ ] 279 Mark 1:16-45; Matthew 4:18-25; 8:2-4, 14-17; Luke 4:31-5:16
- [ ] 280 Matthew 9:1-17; Mark 2:1-22; Luke 5:17-39
- [ ] 281 John 5; Matthew 12:1-21; Mark 2:23-3:12; Luke 6:1-11
- [ ] 282 Matthew 5; Mark 3:13-19; Luke 6:12-36
- [ ] 283 Matthew 6-7; Luke 6:37-49
- [ ] 284 Luke 7; Matthew 8:1, 5-13; 11:2-30
- [ ] 285 Matthew 12:22-50; Mark 3:20-35; Luke 8:1-21
- [ ] 286 Mark 4:1-34; Matthew 13:1-53
- [ ] 287 Mark 4:35-5:43; Matthew 8:18, 23-34; 9:18-34; Luke 8:22-56
- [ ] 288 Mark 6:1-30; Matthew 13:54-58; 9:35-11:1; 14:1-12; Luke 9:1-10

BIBLE READING SCHEDULE

Day 289 - 365

- [ ] 289 Matthew 14:13-36; Mark 6:31-56; Luke 9:11-17; John 6:1-21
- [ ] 290 John 6:22-7:1; Matthew 15:1-20; Mark 7:1-23
- [ ] 291 Matthew 15:21-16:20; Mark 7:24-8:30; Luke 9:18-21
- [ ] 292 Matthew 16:21-17:27; Mark 8:31-9:32; Luke 9:22-45
- [ ] 293 Matthew 18; 8:19-22; Mark 9:33-50; Luke 9:46-62; John 7:2-10
- [ ] 294 John 7:11-8:59
- [ ] 295 Luke 10:1-11:36
- [ ] 296 Luke 11:37-13:21
- [ ] 297 John 9-10
- [ ] 298 Luke 13:22-15:32
- [ ] 299 Luke 16:1-17:10; John 11:1-54
- [ ] 300 Luke 17:11-18:17; Matthew 19:1-15; Mark 10:1-16
- [ ] 301 Matthew 19:16-20:28; Mark 10:17-45; Luke 18:18-34
- [ ] 302 Matthew 20:29-34; 26:6-13; Mark 10:46-52; 14:3-9; Luke 18:35-19:28; John 11:55-12:11
- [ ] 303 Matthew 21:1-22; Mark 11:1-26; Luke 19:29-48; John 12:12-50
- [ ] 304 Matthew 21:23-22:14; Mark 11:27-12:12; Luke 20:1-19
- [ ] 305 Matthew 22:15-46; Mark 12:13-37; Luke 20:20-44
- [ ] 306 Matthew 23; Mark 12:38-44; Luke 20:45-21:4
- [ ] 307 Matthew 24:1-31; Mark 13:1-27; Luke 21:5-27
- [ ] 308 Matthew 24:32-26:5, 14-16; Mark 13:28-14:2, 10-11; Luke 21:28-22:6
- [ ] 309 Matthew 26:17-29; Mark 14:12-25; Luke 22:7-38; John 13
- [ ] 310 John 14-16
- [ ] 311 John 17:1-18:1; Matthew 26:30-46; Mark 14:26-42; Luke 22:39-46
- [ ] 312 Matthew 26:47-75; Mark 14:43-72; Luke 22:47-65; John 18:2-27
- [ ] 313 Matthew 27:1-26; Mark 15:1-15; Luke 22:66-23:25; John 18:28-19:16
- [ ] 314 Matthew 27:27-56; Mark 15:16-41; Luke 23:26-49; John 19:17-30
- [ ] 315 Matthew 27:57-28:8; Mark 15:42-16:8; Luke 23:50-24:12; John 19:31-20:10
- [ ] 316 Matthew 28:9-20; Mark 16:9-20; Luke 24:13-53; John 20:11-21:25
- [ ] 317 Acts 1-2
- [ ] 318 Acts 3-5
- [ ] 319 Acts 6:1-8:1
- [ ] 320 Acts 8:2-9:43
- [ ] 321 Acts 10-11
- [ ] 322 Acts 12-13
- [ ] 323 Acts 14-15
- [ ] 324 Galatians 1-3
- [ ] 325 Galatians 4-6
- [ ] 326 James
- [ ] 327 Acts 16:1-18:11
- [ ] 328 1 Thessalonians
- [ ] 329 2 Thessalonians; Acts 18:12-19:22
- [ ] 330 1 Corinthians 1-4
- [ ] 331 1 Corinthians 5-8
- [ ] 332 1 Corinthians 9-11
- [ ] 333 1 Corinthians 12-14
- [ ] 334 1 Corinthians 15-16
- [ ] 335 Acts 19:23-20:1; 2 Corinthians 1-4
- [ ] 336 2 Corinthians 5-9
- [ ] 337 2 Corinthians 10-13
- [ ] 338 Romans 1-3
- [ ] 339 Romans 4-6
- [ ] 340 Romans 7-8
- [ ] 341 Romans 9-11
- [ ] 342 Romans 12-15
- [ ] 343 Romans 16; Acts 20:2-21:16
- [ ] 344 Acts 21:17-23:35
- [ ] 345 Acts 24-26
- [ ] 346 Acts 27-28
- [ ] 347 Ephesians 1-3
- [ ] 348 Ephesians 4-6
- [ ] 349 Colossians
- [ ] 350 Philippians
- [ ] 351 Philemon; 1 Timothy 1-3
- [ ] 352 1 Timothy 4-6; Titus
- [ ] 353 2 Timothy
- [ ] 354 1 Peter
- [ ] 355 Jude; 2 Peter
- [ ] 356 Hebrews 1:1-5:10
- [ ] 357 Hebrews 5:11-9:28
- [ ] 358 Hebrews 10-11
- [ ] 359 Hebrews 12-13; 2 John; 3 John
- [ ] 360 1 John
- [ ] 361 Revelation 1-3
- [ ] 362 Revelation 4-9
- [ ] 363 Revelation 10-14
- [ ] 364 Revelation 15-18
- [ ] 365 Revelation 19-22

From the Liberty Bible, King James Version.
Copyright ©1975, Thomas Nelson, Inc. Publishers. Used by permission.

WEEK 1

Have you ever asked a friend to keep a secret only to find out they told someone, or, have you needed to talk to someone and they just shrugged you off? This week's passages will focus on the One we can trust and go to at these times. You can fully trust God to be there when you need Him.

PRAYER FOCUS FOR THIS WEEK

THE QUESTION: What is the writer saying?

THE ANSWER: How can I apply this to my life?

SUNDAY • Psalm 120:1-7

DIGGING DEEPER Isolation is a frightening thing. Think of someone in prison who is alone in solitary confinement. Not only is he away from his family and friends, but now he is completely alone. We can also feel alone while being surrounded by people. That is the predicament of the psalmist here. As a person who is trying to walk with God, he feels isolated by being surrounded by those who do not fear Him. But God promises His presence and peace to anyone who determines to follow Him. Even when surrounded by enemies, we can still find peace and comfort in God's presence.

Have you ever felt alone for standing up for what's right? Sometimes we need to remind ourselves that God still cares. Have you tried praying for those who persecute you (Matthew 5:44)?

MONDAY • Psalm 121:1-8

 As long as you have Christ in your life he will watch over you no matter what.

 Make my faith stronger with christ.

DIGGING DEEPER Have you ever been involved in a project for school that seemed impossible? Maybe you felt you didn't have enough time, or maybe you just didn't know what to do. Then maybe a friend came along who offered to help you, and it became so simple you almost felt embarrassed for thinking it was hard? God is the One Who lines up help for us when we need it most. Many times we forget to look for it, and so often we forget to thank Him for His goodness. God also provides comfort and rest (v. 5). God is ultimately in control for both our souls (v. 7) and our physical well-being (v. 8).

Are you keeping your eyes open for where God is helping you? Do you thank Him for these times? How can you look to pass on this help to others?

Sometimes I notice when god helps me. I do not thank him. Tell People about the word of God

TUESDAY • Psalm 122:1-9

 Try in anyway to grow closer to god and try in any way to worship him.

 go to church as much as possible so I can learn his word better.

DIGGING DEEPER It seems as though the headlines today are a never-ending theme of war and trouble and fighting. It may seem like a waste of time to pray for peace. The psalmist was also living in pretty dismal times, but he didn't give up in despair. We need to follow his example and run to God during our trials, not run away from them. God works even through our difficulties (Romans 8:28). Praying for peace will both strengthen us and help us be secure in our relationship with God. It will also go a long way in showing the unsaved that there is a God Who is concerned about them too.

God often brings peace into our personal lives even as the world struggles. How has He done this for you? How can you ask God to give you a peaceful spirit in tough situations? He tries to bring me closer to him by doing devotionals. I can pray.

WEDNESDAY • Psalm 123:1-4

 To depend on god unknow and to follow his word.

 when ever I have a problem I can turn to the bible for guidance.

DIGGING DEEPER A new baby requires the undivided attention of its parents. The baby can do nothing for itself and can only communicate to the outside world by crying. It is totally dependent on someone else to care for its every need. We may look at this and think of it as a sign of weakness, but God wants us to depend on Him just as much! Exercising one's independence of God is an act of rebellion. He doesn't want us to be helpless like a baby, but He does ask us to be, only humble enough to seek Him and even cry out for the help we need. Verse 2 talks about the constant attention we need to give God so we can see how He is leading us to live.

Who or what do you turn to when your heart is troubled? How can you make looking to God (v. 2) part of your everyday life? I turn to none no one because I keep all my trouble to my self.

THURSDAY • Psalm 124:1-8

 Because christ died on the cross, we are free from sin.

 Think more about what christ has done for me

DIGGING DEEPER Have you ever had a class that seemed really difficult for you, but once you got a friend to help you, was easier to understand? David is expressing similar emotions here. He had experienced very difficult trials and escaped with his life. Notice that he gives God the glory for delivering him. There is no place for pride or arrogance, which only allows the evil one to gain a stronghold in our lives. We may not see physical deliverance like David did, but God is always there to help us with our daily struggle with sin.

When you get through a trial, do you thank God? Do you look for Him in the middle of that hard time? Is there anyone you know who is having a hard time and is confused about why it is happening? How can you help them see God?

FRIDAY • Psalm 125:1-5

Q *Be with christ now because when the time comes he will punish all who are not with him.*

A *Try my best to put god in all my situations in life.*

DIGGING DEEPER Sometimes it feels like people get away with doing wrong. The good guy always gets walked on. God seems so far away. Perhaps that is why the psalmist reminds himself that God is on his side and will not let evil win. It might look bleak now, but it will get better. We need to be reminded how Jesus was treated and how He responded. He put others in front of His own feelings and loved them in spite of what was being done to Him. He prayed for them. We must live in hopeful expectation of the world that Jesus will bring when He returns.

Do you feel like the good guy always finishes last? Can you think of present-day examples where wickedness was actually judged? God says following Him will be rewarding; perhaps you need to ask Him to help remind you of that in rough times.

SATURDAY • Psalm 126:1-6

Q *No matter what god will come through and help us in the end.*

A *Yes I know people with hardened hearts and I know god will reach them if they open up theyre hearts.*

DIGGING DEEPER You have probably heard of soldiers who have gone off to war in some strange and far-away land. They felt lost and missed their families and friends and were scared about the uncertainty of maybe never seeing them again. But then they got to go home! Think about the joyful arrival of the Israelite remnant that returned to Jerusalem after being held in captivity in Babylon for 70 years. God takes us into different circumstances for many different reasons, but we can always trust in the harvest at the end (v. 6), where we enjoy the fruit of His plans.

Are there people you know who have hardened hearts and seem impossible to reach for Christ? Have you considered it too difficult for God to reach them?

WEEK 2

Are there times when you think you've achieved a lot spiritually? We need to be reminded that all of our plans, no matter how good our intentions may be, will not be worthwhile if they exclude God. Only those plans that are rooted in trust in God will be blessed by Him.

PRAYER FOCUS FOR THIS WEEK

THE QUESTION: What is the writer saying?
THE ANSWER: How can I apply this to my life?

SUNDAY • Psalm 127:1-5

Q Everything that we do in life must for god of it will be done in vain.

A To apply this to my life I could pot god first and make sure I to not do it in vain.

DIGGING DEEPER You can have the most powerful motor in the world, but without one crucial ingredient, it will never leave the driveway: fuel. It is the same way in our lives. Those who do not know Christ try in vain to find purpose in all the things the world has to offer—money, fame, building great structures, exciting experiences. Unless we are seeking God and what He wants for our lives, though, we will eventually fail. All our earthly efforts leave us empty—a motor without fuel to really go—without the source of life itself: God. He makes our efforts turn into real fruit.

Where are some common places that people place their hope and security? Why do these things bring emptiness? How can you put God in the center of your actions?

MONDAY • Psalm 128:1-6

 As long as you fear God you will be blessed.

 As I grow older try to ~~learn~~ tell other people about ~~the~~ bible

DIGGING DEEPER Have you ever had a teacher who just scared you to death? You heard the horror stories from the older kids about how mean or strict this teacher was. In short, that teacher struck *fear* in you. Is this what the psalmist means by "fear the Lord" in verse 4? "Fear" in this sense means *awe*. When all God has done for us finally clicks in our heads, we are in awe of Him and no longer see ourselves as most important. We praise Him and thank Him. This attitude—this true understanding of Who God is—spreads to other areas of life, such as the home (v. 3).

Have you had moments where you really understand what it means to fear God? Having the knowledge of God actually change our lives can be difficult, but once it does, we will be on the way to a pattern of life (v. 1) that God says is best. Ask God to help you really see Who He is today.

TUESDAY • Psalm 129:1-8

 Because the lord died for us we are free from sin. and as long as we are with god the devil will try to bring us down. But with god on our side he will fail.

DIGGING DEEPER The psalmist is a great example of someone who feared God and, as a result, lived out God's ways in many situations. Here he returns to the subject of hardships. The rough places in the road of life help us strengthen our spiritual muscles. Israel is the prime example (v. 1) of God using difficult times to develop character and help people trust Him. Fearing God, and knowing we need to trust His ways, is just the beginning of the process. Next we need to practice daily trusting Him. As circumstances sap our strength, we learn to lean on Him and see more of Who He is.

Can you think of a trial that you struggled with, yet your faith grew as a result? How did this show you more of Who God is?

DIGGING DEEPER Even when we have a relationship with God, we often get turned around and find ourselves falling back into sin. Another part of fearing God is that as righteous as He is, He also has forgiveness waiting for us when we realize we're wrong (v. 4). Choosing to humble ourselves, admit our sin, and accept this forgiveness helps us know God in a new way. (See Luke 15 for a full story of how God waits for us to come back to Him.) It may be easier for us to "fear" God when we think of Him as a powerful Judge, but these verses show Him as taking us in when our attempts at being good for Him come up short.

Do you ever find that the more you try to do good for God, the farther you come up short? Sometimes God lets us work hard "for Him" so we can realize just how powerless we are and how good He is.

THURSDAY • Psalm 132:1-9

DIGGING DEEPER In these verses, the psalmist writes about finding a proper place for God's ark and tabernacle—physically keeping God in a place of importance. Although God cares only about what's going on in our hearts, the way we act often shows whether we are making God important in our lives. How do you prepare your heart for worshiping the Lord on Sunday morning? Going to church on Sunday should not be some religious duty. We should examine ourselves spiritually to make sure we come with a pure heart with no unconfessed sin. We are told to worship Him both in spirit and truth (John 4:24).

Do you pray for your church service before it begins? Why do you think it is important that you don't come to worship with a polluted spirit? What do you do to make sure that your time with God is given special attention?

FRIDAY • Psalm 132:10-18

DIGGING DEEPER Each of us has been the victim of someone who has broken a promise to us. You can recall the hurt and disappointment you felt from it and how it was hard to trust that person. When God promises something, we can be sure it will happen. For Christians, God promises to change us to be more like Him as we follow His instructions. For David, the promises were physically tangible—God promised that His throne would be established forever. Jesus, a descendant of David, was the fulfillment of God's promise!

Why do you think it is important for God to keep His promises? What difference would it make if He decided to change His mind?

SATURDAY • Psalms 133:1 – 134:3

DIGGING DEEPER Often when we think of peace, fighting, and divisions, we think of warring nations in the Middle East. We seldom associate these words with the church. But when believers lose themselves to selfish pride, they often act worse than the unsaved. God tells us to seek unity, not division. Proving who is right isn't important. We should unite together in love to serve God (not ourselves) in ways we could never serve if left to ourselves alone. Senseless divisiveness inhibits God's work.

What are some practical ways you've seen unity help the church? How about selfishness or pride hurting it? How can you change the way you treat people?

WEEK 3

The words that so freely pass through our lips should be measured with care. Better yet, they should give praise and thanksgiving to God, Who has generously given to us in many ways, both spiritually and physically. Look for different things for which to praise Him in this week's passages.

PRAYER FOCUS FOR THIS WEEK

THE QUESTION: What is the writer saying?

THE ANSWER: How can I apply this to my life?

SUNDAY • Psalm 135:1-12

DIGGING DEEPER What makes Christianity different from the other world religions? Let's start with the fact that we worship a living God, and that God wants to develop a personal relationship with us! Other religions worship someone who has died and stayed dead or something else (idols) that are unable to hear and respond. In these verses, the psalmist constantly calls attention to God's name. A person's name is what their reputation hangs on. When we hear certain names, we think of very specific characteristics. What comes to mind when you hear Alexander the Great, Robin Hood, Billy Graham, or Serena Williams? Pretty different, huh? What comes to mind when you hear the different names of God?

How different is the way you think of God in everyday life from Who He says He is in the Bible? Do your circumstances affect how you see Him?

MONDAY • Psalm 135:13-21

DIGGING DEEPER We may know only a few people who worship actual idols, but plenty of us have other idols in our lives (v. 15). Objects, hobbies, or people become more important than God, or we spend more time pursuing them. Have you ever struggled with giving too much attention to TV, a favorite sport, or a close friend or girlfriend/boyfriend? Look at verse 18. When we elevate something that is less than God and try to be satisfied by it, we become like it—inferior—rather than becoming like God.

Can you think of specific idols in your life? How about activities that are easier to do or understand than to spend time with God? Do you need to spend more time learning about Who God is?

TUESDAY • Psalm 136:1-9

DIGGING DEEPER Why does the psalmist repeat the same phrase over and over? A couple reasons: 1) It's true, 2) Being sung, as psalms were, it's having the singer sing a verse, and the people replying with the familiar chorus. Think about verses 5-9 and see what it says about creation. The psalmist puts a lot of emphasis on where we come from because that's the key to life today—God created us for specific reasons. His act of creation shows us that the history of the world and even your life today, is not because of chance. Our only response should be to worship, acknowledging that from the beginning of the world and throughout each day, "His mercy endures forever" (v. 1-4).

How does knowing God created the earth affect your life today? Can you share this hope with someone else?

WEDNESDAY • Psalm 136:10-26

DIGGING DEEPER Now that you are familiar with the repeating pattern of the psalm, try going through it and reading just the first half of each verse to see the picture that it describes. You will soon realize that God is on our side. Have you ever felt like the underdog? That it was you against everyone else or really tough circumstances? That must have been how tiny Israel must have felt numerous times. Yet God intervened to help His people in their time of need. Praise Him that He has provided us with the bread of life so that we will never hunger spiritually but will always be satisfied (John 6:35).

Is there an impossible situation you are going through now? Can you see God's hand in it? Search for it, because it's there!

THURSDAY • Psalm 137:1-9

DIGGING DEEPER Have you ever tried singing or laughing when you're not happy? It's no easy task. It goes against our natural tendencies. Israel was in bondage, and there was no joy. Enemies were going to tear down the walls of the Israelites' main city, Jerusalem. Israel's only hope was that the Lord would see its plight and take care of its enemies. Has anyone ever done anything to hurt your feelings? Did you ever catch yourself daydreaming of how sweet revenge was going to be? You know that these feelings of bitterness, rage, and resentment are wrong, but you feel like that wrong will go unnoticed. It won't. God sees and knows what those people have done. It is up to Him and Him alone to judge them.

Do you find it difficult to forgive those who have wronged you, especially those who don't apologize? Are there people you need to apologize to?

FRIDAY • Psalm 138:1-8

DIGGING DEEPER The psalmist can't escape the truth that God's mercy "endures forever." Friends fail, and life serves lemons, but God's mercy is still there. Learn to trust God to sweeten things up and serve the world lemonade! Are there times when you feel that absolutely nothing you can do would make God accept you? Good! There isn't anything you can do to earn God's favor through human efforts. God knows each of us, and all our terrible parts, yet He still loves us and accepts us no matter what. Isn't that reason enough to praise Him? He gives strength to those who are weak and humble. He resuscitates those who are clinging to life.

David is praying for specific help here, but he also points out many things about God. List some of them. Do you reflect on these things when praying for God's help?

SATURDAY • Psalm 139:1-12

DIGGING DEEPER Ever felt like trying to escape or hide from God? Jonah tried, but it didn't work (see Jonah 1). In today's passage, the psalmist admits that there's nowhere on earth He can go and not be led by God's hand (vv. 9-10). How about your thoughts (v. 2)? How does it feel to realize God knows all our motives, wherever you've been (v. 3), and whether you mean what you say (v. 4)? On one hand, we may not like the idea of a "Big Brother" knowing what we're doing all the time, but on the other, this is a reassuring thought when we remind ourselves that God is truly good and caring.

Is there something God already knows but you need to confess to Him? If there is something you feel God is asking you to do, then do it.

WEEK 4

We weaken when our focus shifts off of God and to our circumstances. God is all-powerful, and since He lives in us through the Holy Spirit, His power helps us resist the lures of sin. This week we will see four of David's prayers asking God to hear his requests, set up some restraints, and provide refuge.

PRAYER FOCUS FOR THIS WEEK

THE QUESTION: What is the writer saying?

THE ANSWER: How can I apply this to my life?

SUNDAY • Psalm 139:13-24

DIGGING DEEPER These verses are pretty clear in saying that man is fully known by God. That alone is a big statement about God. Yet He not only knows everything about us, but He also wants to communicate with us. This is more than David can comprehend! He is struggling here to put this together in his head—why such a powerful God would want to know us. The psalmist asks God to search him so he can see the things that are keeping him from knowing God more fully. Sometimes people are one of the things between us and God (vv. 19-22).

Are you afraid to ask God to search your heart because of what He may find? Does it comfort or scare you that He knows so much about you?

MONDAY • Psalm 140:1-13

DIGGING DEEPER When we walk in the world, there's a natural tendency to get dirty, both physically and spiritually. The world, with all its cares, clutter, and carnality only makes it more difficult. A lot of the stuff going on in the world today—wars, hunger, violence—may make you wonder why God sometimes seems to be asleep at the wheel. David called on God to intervene and punish his enemies. What God is trying to teach us here is to communicate with Him and to leave the results to Him. Who better to handle the situation than the God Who created us and knows everything about us?

Why not express your appreciation to God right now for not punishing your every instance of disobedience? Can you think of someone you need to forgive or seek forgiveness from since God has so freely forgiven you?

TUESDAY • Psalm 141:1-10

DIGGING DEEPER David asks God to guard his speech and his heart. Both have a tendency to betray us. The wise person is open to receiving rebuke and instruction from mature believers. In verses 4-5, David shows the difference between being around the righteous and associating with the wicked. This world lusts after its own way and wants to live for itself. But David wants all of his ways to be pleasing to God.

Do you desire to do the right thing even when it isn't popular? Has your prayer life become cold? Try praying some of David's requests back to the Lord, inserting some personal items.

WEDNESDAY • Psalm 142:1-7

DIGGING DEEPER Have you ever tried living in a cave? It's one thing to be there for a campout, but to use it as a place of refuge when there is no other place to go is something different. Have you ever felt like you're in a cave and asked God to find you a way out? When we are overwhelmed by circumstances, it's easy to think God is obligated to provide a way out. But often, He lets us taste the bitterness of hardship. We learn to trust and rely on God most when we struggle and can't make it on our own. As verse 5 says, *He* becomes our refuge.

What cave are you looking for a way out of? Could God be allowing you to stay to develop your faith in Him? When do you feel closer to God—when things are going well, or not so well?

THURSDAY • Psalm 143:1-12

DIGGING DEEPER David asks God to be patient with him. He has lost everything materially and might as well be dead. He is tired of making excuses and is now willing to take a moment to reflect and remember the good times when he knew firsthand of God's faithfulness. Thinking about God causes him to offer praise. Soon he has a new thirst for God and His Word. He wants to hear from God again and experience His nearness and the victory over sin in his life. That's the true sign of a person who is developing and maturing spiritually. In the last six verses, there are 11 requests of God. Can you find them? God wants to hear from you.

How exciting is your quiet time with God? Why? Do you feel empty inside if you skip reading the Bible for a day? Why not make it a matter of prayer?

FRIDAY • Psalm 144:1-15

DIGGING DEEPER If this psalm sounds familiar, it's because it's a compilation of verses from five previous psalms. It is a king's prayer asking for victory and blessing. When we place ourselves in a position of dependency on God, we can pray and ask for help. Notice the kind of prayers that are here. We sometimes pray for God to supply our material prosperity, as if that alone would bring true happiness. But God has different, more substantial ways of providing for us. True happiness comes with the realization that our true enemy has been defeated and that Heaven and an eternal inheritance await us.

Do you depend on God? If so, what are you asking God to do for you today?

SATURDAY • Psalm 145:1-9

DIGGING DEEPER This final psalm of David is called a psalm of praise. Every verse shares something for which God is praiseworthy. Many of these are areas where we can still praise God today. Think about the last time you got a really great gift, and how you felt. Shouldn't we be doing the same with God and the Gospel? The Person and the gift should be proclaimed from the rooftops!

Are you excited about your gift of salvation? Where would you be if the person who shared the Gospel with you wasn't excited about it and witnessed freely? Who can you share with today?

WEEK 5

We easily become faint and lose heart. Like Peter walking on the water, once he looked away from Jesus and at the waves around him, he lost his focus and began to sink. These last few psalms beginning with Psalm 146, all start and end with "Praise ye the Lord." Let's focus on Him, not our trials!

PRAYER FOCUS FOR THIS WEEK

THE QUESTION: What is the writer saying?

THE ANSWER: How can I apply this to my life?

SUNDAY • Psalm 145:10-21

DIGGING DEEPER As this psalm concludes, we are given a few more reasons why God is worthy to be praised. In verse 14, He promises help for all those that fall—that means there's hope for us! Look at verse 18. Can you remember a time when you saw a child separated from his mother? Do you remember how he cried out? God hears our cries and rescues us. He brings us into His safety, and all fear is cast out. Jesus has found and rescued us.

Do you ever feel lost, abandoned, or alone? Can you remember when God came and found you—or have you never really met God and had a relationship with Him?

MONDAY • Psalm 146:1-10

DIGGING DEEPER This is the beginning of the five "Hallelujah" Psalms. They all start and end with "Praise ye the Lord." Verse 3 points to the things we often trust. If you have to choose between God, man, or money, choose God every time. Man is flawed and, as hard as he tries, can't be trusted like God can. They fatally believe that things can bring them happiness and respect, similar to the wealthy man who had way more than he needed and decided to build bigger barns to store his grain and goods (Luke 12:16-21). When we put either of these above our love for God, we are guilty of idolatry (1 Timothy 6:10). God knows what we need, so we should not feel jealous of those who have more than we do.
Would having all you ever wanted make and keep you happy? How can you use some of what you have to help others and bring glory to God?

TUESDAY • Psalm 147:1-11

DIGGING DEEPER The psalmist returns to the theme of fearing God (v. 11), with each verse before describing why God should be feared and praised. God is the mighty Creator Who has even named the stars (v. 4). He is powerful and understanding in everything (v. 5). He values humility—people who know their place before Him—and punishes wickedness (v. 6). He takes care of the earth daily, renewing life (v. 8). Above all, the God we are called to fear does not look at human, physical qualities like we do. He wants people who realize He's got it all (v. 11) and wants people who are willing to accept His gift of mercy. He enjoys healing our wounds and making up for our insufficiencies (v. 3).
Do you ever get caught up in thinking how much you have to offer? Not compared to God! He calls us to let Him be God, and to enjoy His mercy.

WEDNESDAY • Psalm 147:12-20

DIGGING DEEPER   This psalm was probably written to celebrate the rebuilding of the wall in Jerusalem in Nehemiah's day. The Jews had to deal with intense criticism as they worked (Nehemiah 4:2). Yet they kept doing what was right and turned their backs on the sinful persuasion of their attackers. We need to be ready for criticism as we follow God. When things are going smooth for any length of time, be alert—there may be some rough road ahead. The key to being ready is preparing ahead. Any athlete knows that the game is won in practice. The more prepared you become, the more skilled you are in the actual game.
Have you ever stood up for what was right only to be made fun of? Has anyone ridiculed your faith in Christ? What can you do to prepare yourself to respond well?

THURSDAY • Psalm 148:1-14

DIGGING DEEPER   All of creation offers praise to God. It all reflects the God that made it—except man. We often fall short in this area. We're no different than Israel—we soon forget God's goodness and remain silent even though creation shouts out His praises. God is asking for a lifestyle of praise here—not just worship time on Sunday mornings but a life of praising Him every day, both in words and actions. His Word has instructions on how to feed ourselves so we can mature and thrive in our relationship with Him.
How can you daily spend time offering God praise for all He has done for you? If this is difficult, ask God to really help you see practically why He should be praised.

FRIDAY • Psalm 149:1-9

DIGGING DEEPER People worship and praise God differently. Some ways we feel comfortable with and some we don't. What does God want? Well, what do you think God thinks about this? In verse 3, they're using a harp, and in verse 4, the writer says God finds pleasure in humble people. The best way we can praise God is in our attitude toward Him. Once we put Him first, we can be sensitive to His leading about how to act, and worship, in different situations.

How do you think you can make your time worshiping God fresh? How can you remind yourself of Who God really is? Ask God to help your attitude and lifestyle become a thing of worship.

SATURDAY • Psalm 150:1-8

DIGGING DEEPER What does "everything that has breath praise the Lord" really mean? This psalm goes through a bunch of different ways of praising God with many instruments for His power and greatness. The psalmist is saying that anything on earth that has movement or breath only has it because of God. Basic life, and everything after that—excitement, talents, enjoyment, time—come out of a God Who has a personality and a reason for making all these things. Often, the ways we try to worship God are limited to simple songs or an obvious act, such as giving money. God calls us to find creative ways to praise Him.

If God gives everything—life, time, abilities, and even joy—where in your life should you be showing Him praise? Perhaps in the same places He works in you? Can you think of new ways to reflect glory back to Him?

WEEK 6

1 Timothy is like a letter to a good buddy. A young pastor needs instruction on how to handle problems at his church. His best friend writes him and gives him help. The funny thing is, the problems are the same things we struggle with. God has something just for you this week!

PRAYER FOCUS FOR THIS WEEK

THE QUESTION: What is the writer saying?

THE ANSWER: How can I apply this to my life?

SUNDAY • 1 Timothy 1:1-11

DIGGING DEEPER Timothy was a young pastor in a city called Ephesus. Paul was the guy who helped Timothy grow as a Christian for many years. Paul wrote to help Timothy handle some problems in the church. The biggest problem was that people in the church were not teaching God's Word correctly. In fact, they were stirring up trouble and arguments. Even Timothy, a pastor, needed help knowing how to deal with this. But all of us could use help in our Christian walk. Everyone needs a *Paul* in his life—an older Christian who can help us grow and live like God wants us to.

Who is the Paul in your Christian walk? Do you have a great desire to learn from him or her? If you don't have someone, what can you do to find someone to help you grow?

MONDAY • 1 Timothy 1:12-20

DIGGING DEEPER Don't you wish you knew where some buried treasure was? These verses show us that if we know Christ, we already have the greatest treasure in the world. We sometimes forget that Christ and His promises are such a great thing, but Paul is a good example of someone who was rightly thankful. Paul knew he was a sinner, and that somehow, although he didn't deserve it, Christ pardoned all his sin. How precious is your salvation to you? Yes, we're glad we're saved, but are we thankful enough to be unquestionably faithful to our Lord? If you measure your thankfulness by your commitment to God, how thankful are you, really? We could all be more grateful!
Would you commit to thanking the Lord for your salvation throughout the day? Can people see your thankfulness in your dedication to God?

TUESDAY • 1 Timothy 2:1-8

DIGGING DEEPER Paul is giving some instruction on how prayer should work in the church. We ought to ask for the needs of others, worship God, and also express thankfulness. The key element in prayer is understanding that Christ made it all possible. No one comes to God, His salvation, or His blessings except through Christ. That's why we often pray "in Jesus' name." Paul reminds us that Jesus died for *all* people. In Timothy's church, there were some enemies. But Paul says we should pray for everyone, even people with whom we are having problems. If Christ died for all people, we must pray for all people.
With whom are you having a conflict right now? Are you praying for God to help him or her, and to help you resolve it? Who can you add to your prayer list who does not know Christ?

WEDNESDAY • 1 Timothy 2:9-15

DIGGING DEEPER Apparently there were some ladies causing problems in the church. These women were concerned about the way they looked on the outside. Paul said that more important than physically looking good is spiritually— to be dressed up with "good works." The inside is what counts! The other inward problem these women struggled with was humility. We all need to be submissive and humble. Even Christ was submissive to His Father's will. These women were more concerned about causing trouble than about learning. Learning is such an important part of the Christian life because this is how we know God. It's hard to learn if we're the ones doing all the talking!

Are you more concerned about your outward appearance than your heart attitude toward God? Are you the kind of person who is eager to learn?

THURSDAY • 1 Timothy 3:1-7

DIGGING DEEPER Are you the kind of person who likes to be in charge? Be careful—leadership is not easy! There were people in Timothy's church who wanted to be pastors. That's good, but such an important role has some requirements. One of the biggest ones is to be "blameless." Pastors need to be the people you can't point the finger at and accuse of living wrong. That means they need to be very mature spiritually, and not new (or a "novice") to the Christian walk. How can they help someone else grow if they haven't first been growing for many years? Leadership is about being the right person, not being in the right position.

Is being in charge more important to you than being a godly person? What should you change in order to be a godly leader someday?

FRIDAY • 1 Timothy 3:8-16

DIGGING DEEPER Yesterday we looked at what a pastor ought to be. Today we're looking at another position in the church: the deacon. The key word to remember about a deacon is *servant*. These are people who are to be directly under the pastor, but who do whatever is necessary to serve the church. These people are vital in the church today. They don't necessarily run things, but they help the pastor and the church accomplish its mission by serving God and serving others. There's no job too low for them. They'll do whatever it takes to make it happen. This may sound like a dirty job, but God says it is a great honor to serve in a local church. Maybe we're not all deacons yet, but we all should be willing to serve others.
Would you be willing to pick two ways you can serve someone today? Are you willing to do *any* job that will help others?

SATURDAY • 1 Timothy 4:1-8

DIGGING DEEPER Ever watch the Olympics? Olympians are chiseled athletes who perform at the highest level. They only compete every four years, so what do they do for four years while they wait? TRAIN! They work out and get ready. The same things should be true of Christians, except our Olympics are every day! We discipline ourselves inside and out to live godly lives. That's just the opposite of what some people were doing at Timothy's church. They were teaching lies and training people to follow ungodly rules instead of following Christ. Our training schedule includes disciplines such as quiet time, Scripture memory, church attendance, prayer, Christian service, and learning God's Word!
Are you giving God a half-hearted effort in your Christian training? Have you been training yourself to be ungodly?

WEEK 7

Life would be really fun if it weren't for people, right? Parents, teachers, bosses, and everybody else messes up our fun. Timothy had tough people to deal with, too. You'll see it this week, and we'll end with a big-time issue: MONEY! How do you handle it, and what do you do with it? Check it out—you may be surprised!

PRAYER FOCUS FOR THIS WEEK

THE QUESTION: What is the writer saying?

THE ANSWER: How can I apply this to my life?

SUNDAY • 1 Timothy 4:9-16

DIGGING DEEPER "People don't trust me!" "Nobody thinks I can make a difference!" Do you ever think thoughts like this? Timothy may have. If Timothy was to get anything from this letter, this is what Paul wanted him to remember! The message is basically this: Just keep doing what a pastor is supposed to be doing. Even if people look down on you, just keep teaching the Word. Set the right example for everyone (v. 12). Make sure you believe and teach exactly what God says. People can criticize us, but if we are being faithful to God in all aspects of our lives, their words will have little effect. Our job is to be faithful to God's Word and God's work. That is our focus!

Is there any area of your life in which you're not being faithful? Are you focusing on your critics or on pleasing God?

MONDAY • 1 Timothy 5:1-8

DIGGING DEEPER Because some of Timothy's critics were older men, Paul gave him some instruction on how to be respectful to them while still correcting biblical error. Sometimes it's hard to be respectful to adults, especially ones who may not be kind to you. We must avoid stooping to their level. Paul describes the people in a church as family, though. Paul assumes that we treat our own families with respect, love, and care. Paul talks about women whose husbands have died, leaving them all alone. But if these widows have a family, they will be taken care of. Consider verse 8 when it comes to taking care of brothers, sisters, and other members of your family.

How do you treat your brothers and sisters? Is it honoring to God? Do you honor and care for your parents and grandparents?

TUESDAY • 1 Timothy 5:9-16

DIGGING DEEPER So what's the big deal with widows? This was an important issue at this church. If a widow didn't have any family, the church was supposed to take care of her. This included food, water, housing, medicine, and everything else. Some widows could have just been looking for free help. It was pretty common for people to lose their health, die young, or get diseases in those days. Timothy needed these guidelines so he could encourage the church to take care of the widows who needed the most help. Some people try to get free stuff instead of working for it. Families need to take care of their own, instead of looking for shortcuts.

A big part of Jesus' message was about looking to care for those around us who need help the most. Look at James 1:27 and Matthew 6:1-4. Can you think of people around you every day who need your help?

DIGGING DEEPER Paul now gives Timothy some advice about the other pastors at the church. Faithful pastors deserve special honor. What's up with the ox? It may sound gross, but farmers had oxen walk over and crush grain so it could be used for cooking. The point is, if the ox is crushing the grain; let him eat some while he's working. He deserves it. Likewise, make sure the pastor is taken care of financially and physically. He works for the Lord! Paul tells Timothy to take a little wine as medicine. In those days, a little wine was a physical remedy. Alcohol used in this way would not be offensive to others or harmful to Timothy's body.

Would you be willing to do something special for your pastor to show him honor? Would you commit to praying for him and his difficult job?

THURSDAY • 1 Timothy 6:1-8

DIGGING DEEPER Slavery? Whoa! In the Bible? This actually isn't the same kind of slavery you may think of. First, these people were more like servant workers. But Paul did want to make sure the relationship between the two Christians was correct. Check out Ephesians 6:7-9 for more understanding. In verse 6, Paul moves on to the question of contentment. Do you feel like you need something else to make you happy? Verse 7 says godly people will be content and satisfied, no matter what they have. These false teachers were always after "more." The point is, we can be completely satisfied with Christ alone. Does He still bless us? Yes! And for that we can be grateful, thankful, and content with what we have.

Are you a faithful worker? Do you always do your best? Are you willing to be satisfied with what you have? What should really bring you happiness?

FRIDAY • 1 Timothy 6:9-16

DIGGING DEEPER What's valuable to you? Verses 9-10 or 15-16? Money or the Messiah? That should be an easy question to answer. At least we know the right answer, but is the right answer really true of us? Paul points out the problems money can cause here in contrast to what God offers. Money is the ticket to earthly things—money, fame, friends, possessions, power—but God is the root of eternal satisfaction. God says what He offers is the best and worth pursuing, but we'll quickly get distracted if money becomes too important.
What do you spend your time thinking about most? What do you spend your time pursuing the most? Can you see what is at the root of that—God or money?

SATURDAY • 1 Timothy 6:17-21

DIGGING DEEPER Do you want to be rich? Actually, you *can* be. But the question is what is important to you in the future? Where is your hope? If it is in God, He can still bless you here on earth. Verse 17 even promises we'll enjoy ourselves. But what God has beyond this earth is even greater. That's why He calls us to good deeds—He knows the only way to prepare for that life is to become more like Him now. By following His instructions, we make it so He can change us. What God calls us to do on this earth is all designed to make us ready for a great life in eternity with Him. He is changing us, but that doesn't mean this life won't be fun.
How about your attitude today? Do you live with this end in mind? Eternity should affect your outlook, your good works, your enjoyment, and your life!

Have you ever wondered what to look for in a friend, what gives a person true value, or even how to be prosperous in life? This week in Proverbs we'll look at these questions and find answers to other everyday questions. We'll even find out how to tell the difference between wise and foolish people.

PRAYER FOCUS FOR THIS WEEK

THE QUESTION: What is the writer saying?
THE ANSWER: How can I apply this to my life?

SUNDAY • Proverbs 26:1-16

DIGGING DEEPER Have you ever read some parts of Proverbs and said, "Duh, *that's* obvious!"? Other times it takes a little more thought to get at the meaning. That's because a proverb is a general truth. Verses 4 and 5 seem to contradict each other. Solomon says in verse 4 that there are times we should not answer a fool because he doesn't really care what we think, and we will lower ourselves to his level. Other times we should answer so he won't go around thinking highly of himself and further harming others. How do you know the difference? Becoming wise and reading the book of Proverbs is a great start. At the end of our passage today we see some reminders of the crazy excuses lazy people use.

Some of the hardest parts of being wise involve knowing how to deal with people. How can you ask God for help in this area today?

MONDAY • Proverbs 26:17-28

DIGGING DEEPER Have you ever tried to break up a fight only to have both people turn on you? How about having a practical joke backfire? Solomon gives a severe warning against deceiving people and then telling them you were just kidding. The rest of the passage today deals with controlling the tongue. First, we are told not to pass on rumors—this reveals our heart problem of not caring about the people we talk about. On the other hand, sometimes we misuse our tongue and give flattering remarks to people and really don't mean it. Solomon warns us that this is not only bad because it is untrue but also because it will harm us in the long run.

Today's passage looked at some things we probably do all the time without thinking. Solomon says these actions can really hurt people, though. Do any of them stick out to you as something you need to change?

TUESDAY • Proverbs 27:1-9

DIGGING DEEPER What are your friends like? What kind of friend are you? Today's passage deals with these questions. In verses 1-2, we see someone who is humble. Those people don't boast about themselves because they are secure in who they are before God. When you know who you are, there is no reason to be jealous of others. Next, Solomon says a friend is open to correction, both to give and receive it. Throughout Proverbs we see that a fool rejects correction and a wise person seeks it. A good friend does the loving thing to help us overcome our faults for the glory of God.

Humility and being a good friend start with us understanding our place before God. Ask God to help you learn about Him today, and to show you specific situations where you can be a good friend to others.

WEDNESDAY • Proverbs 27:10-18

DIGGING DEEPER Remember the little song about the wise man building his house on the rock and a foolish man building his on the sand? That is the contrast we find in today's passage. First, let's look at the foolish man. A fool makes bad decisions because he has not thought out all the consequences of the choice he is making. A fool is loud. A fool makes a terrible spouse, constantly complaining about everything around him or her. A fool offends people by not thinking through what he is saying. A wise person, on the other hand, is loyal. You can count on him to help when and where needed and to say the right thing. A wise person will care for those who are in authority over him.

These verses probably bring to mind some people you know or areas of your own life that are foolish. Ask God to show you ways to be wise today.

THURSDAY • Proverbs 27:19-27

DIGGING DEEPER What do you want to be when you grow up? Do you get tired of answering that question? Most people don't know the answer until they graduate from college; some change their minds later in life and do something totally different. Solomon tells us that part of man's problem is that he is never satisfied with what he has (v. 20). Verses 21-27 explain that only wisdom, and preparing for our ultimate future, will satisfy. Everything else is foolishness.

A major theme in Proverbs is that while earthly riches fade, God provides for the wise and the righteous. Are you satisfied with what God has given you? Why or why not?

DIGGING DEEPER A clear conscience allows you great freedom in the Christian walk and allows you to have real boldness. Think back to a time when you did something wrong. Did you listen differently and look around, expecting to be caught? When you confess and come clean with God, everything is different. You don't have to worry about being found out. There is nothing wrong with being rich, but it is wrong to make money by taking advantage of the poor. Verse 13 is one of the most well-known passages in the book. If a person looks to cover his sin, he will not prosper. Why? Verse 1 says he will live in turmoil, wondering when he will be caught.

Examine your heart and confess any sin you find there. How often do you use what God has given you to thank Him or help others?

SATURDAY • Proverbs 28:15-28

DIGGING DEEPER What does it mean to *prosper*? In the passage today, Solomon contrasts people who live for God with people who live by taking advantage of others. Both will get what they deserve for how they live. If you work hard and look out for the needs of those less fortunate; if you give God all the credit for giving you the abilities to do right, you will prosper. On the other hand, if you are selfish, lazy, and looking out for "number one," God will pay you back for that, too. You may have some money, but your heart won't be right. Which is more important to you?

Give God the credit for the things He's allowed you to accomplish. Confess to Him any selfishness in your heart. Ask Him to help you really see whether you are helping others.

WEEK 9

Have you ever wanted to ask someone for advice on how to deal with people? This week we'll learn how to recognize those opposed to God, how to treat the opposite sex, and things to look for in a future mate. There's a wealth of wisdom waiting to be learned!

PRAYER FOCUS FOR THIS WEEK

THE QUESTION: What is the writer saying?

THE ANSWER: How can I apply this to my life?

SUNDAY • Proverbs 29:1-14

DIGGING DEEPER Have you noticed there are principles repeated throughout Scripture? We learn best by repetition—remember flash cards in grade school? The first principle we see today is about a person who is often rebuked and just stops listening. Not a good idea. Ignoring instruction will ruin him. We see the same thing in verse 5; our poor choices will just trip ourselves up. Another principle repeatedly found in Scripture is that of reaping what you sow (Galatians 6). Evil people sow wickedness, and the result is disastrous. Those who make godly choices will experience blessings because they will reap what is right and good. The Lord is returning and will reward His faithful followers!

Have you been rebuked lately? Listen! We need to thank God for these teaching opportunities and look to become wise.

MONDAY • Proverbs 29:15-27

DIGGING DEEPER When was the last time you thanked your parents for disciplining you? You're probably saying, "Are you kidding? Never!" You will notice throughout Scripture that parents are told to discipline their children. If they don't, the result will bring shame back to them. Another principle mentioned here is thinking before you speak. A person who doesn't think before he talks makes a fool of himself. There are times in life when we need to speak out, but we should think beforehand and pick our words carefully. Satan will tempt us not to say anything, or to use the wrong words, but we need to ignore his putting fear in our hearts.
Do you need to thank your parents for their correction in your life? How about when it's time for us to say something to others? What areas do you need God's help in for speaking wisely?

TUESDAY • Proverbs 30:1-10

DIGGING DEEPER Agur is the author of this Proverb. He was a humble man (vv. 2-4). He teaches us to see that when we open the Bible, we have the pure words of God, with nothing added. (Check out Isaiah 55:11, another great passage about how sufficient Scripture is.) Verses 7-9 have one of the most sincere prayer requests in the entire Bible. When was the last time you heard someone asking God not to make him rich? Agur's fear was that if he got rich, he wouldn't trust God enough. Sometimes God keeps us in the place of having just enough financially so we remember to look at the most important part of life: Him.
Think of some times in your life when you trusted God the most. Was it a time of hardship? Was someone you loved suffering? Did you have a physical need? Why do you think you trusted God then?

WEDNESDAY • Proverbs 30:11-20

DIGGING DEEPER Does it sound like the writer lives in your part of the world? The first four verses sound like a commentary on our culture. Look at the signs of a generation opposed to God's will. First, they curse their parents and are not thankful. A second area is that they think they are OK—that there's nothing wrong. If we compare ourselves with the Word of God, we know we are sinners in need of grace. But when we compare ourselves with others, we tend to be proud and think we are okay. Finally, the people in these verses are a generation that is vicious to those who are not like them. Does that sound like our society to you?
Check your heart and see if any of these signs of opposition to God are in your life somewhere.

THURSDAY • Proverbs 30:21-33

DIGGING DEEPER In this passage, the writer highlights some things that are out of order in the way the world usually works. In verses 24-28, he points to some parts of creation that look too small or helpless but accomplish big things. The writer praises effort such as planning, being safe, teamwork, and working skillfully. Verses 29-31 talk about how we present ourselves. Verse 32 warns against trying to make ourselves look to be more than we really are. Pushing against the natural order and trying to take over (vv. 22-24) rather than working hard and in unity (vv. 24-28) only results in bloody-nose trouble!
A theme of the Bible is that God creates us each for specific purposes, and He will elevate us when it is time. Have you been trying to get ahead or make yourself more important? What can you learn from verses 25-28?

FRIDAY • Proverbs 31:1-9

DIGGING DEEPER Do you remember all the lessons your mother has taught you? Probably not! King Lemuel's mother taught her son three important life lessons. The first deals with how to treat women. In teen terms today, he was not to be a "player" by treating relationships with girls like a sport. Secondly, she deals with drinking alcohol and how it would hinder his ability to make wise decisions. The last lesson was to be wise when dealing with people. He was to treat people according to God's principles, speaking up for the less fortunate, and not by how much popularity or money they had.

This instruction is very practical for life today. Can you write down a specific area where you could use this advice—maybe something you've experienced recently?

SATURDAY • Proverbs 31:10-31

DIGGING DEEPER Guys, what kind of girl catches your interest? Girls, what kind of person are you? King Lemuel describes four principles of an excellent wife that would be great to see in anyone's life. First we see loyalty. She was trusted by her husband and in the community. Next we see that she was an industrious worker. She worked hard with her hands, knew where to get the best bargains, and planned ahead for her family. Third, she was modest and didn't look for attention for herself. She was kind in how she spoke to others and looked out for the less fortunate. Finally, she was godly. She feared God and walked closely with Him.

Pick one of these principles (loyalty, hard worker, modest, godly) to develop or expand in your life.

WEEK 10

When someone has surgery, he's usually grateful he can depend on the surgeon to do the job right. We want someone with experience who won't quit in the middle of the operation. This week we will learn the value of the master surgeon of the spiritual life—the integrity of God's Word and the servants who live by it.

PRAYER FOCUS FOR THIS WEEK

THE QUESTION: What is the writer saying?

THE ANSWER: How can I apply this to my life?

SUNDAY • Galatians 1:1-9

DIGGING DEEPER A deserter weakens any army, hurts morale, and undermines the authority of the officers in charge. Desertion is so serious that, in some cases throughout history, deserters have been imprisoned, shot, or hung. In the opening verses to this book, Paul uses a strong description of the Galatians' actions, saying that he marvels at how quickly they've removed themselves from the Gospel, turning to a false gospel taught by people perverting the Word of God. Paul writes this letter with the intention of turning this process around (5:1), reminding the churches of the influence that Scripture should have on them, and citing the authority of the Gospel he had already taught them (vv. 8-9).
Can you remember a time when you have chosen to follow the truth of Scripture rather than the false teachings you hear throughout the day?

DIGGING DEEPER Reputation. Everybody has one. Our reputation is determined by our character, and everyone sees it and judges it. Paul depends on his reputation as he answers his critics, who claimed that he was teaching one thing to the Jews and something different to the Gentiles. Paul did not receive the Gospel message from men (vv. 11-12) or from the apostles (vv. 16-17). His teaching came directly from Jesus Christ. Paul had a close relationship with the believers in Galatia, and because they knew him, he could depend on his reputation to remind them that his authority came from God, not from man.

Even within Christianity, people try to speak on different authorities—a certain pastor's view, maybe, or one denomination's take. Why is it important to have God's authority behind what we teach?

DIGGING DEEPER When someone spends money on something of value, he wants to know he is getting the genuine article—the *real deal*. Everything from diamonds to vases to paintings and even currency is tested to prove that it is real. In today's passage, Paul defends his teaching and presents evidence that he ministers to people because of the authority given him by Christ, not from other apostles. Paul's message was genuine. This fact was supported by the people who rejoiced that Paul no longer persecuted Christians but instead preached the very faith he once sought to destroy (vv. 22-24). Paul's change of heart and his subsequent teaching were, in fact, the *real deal*.

People knew Paul's preaching was rooted in Christ because his life was being changed by Christ. What is God doing in your life today?

WEDNESDAY • Galatians 2:1-6

DIGGING DEEPER Anyone who learns a new skill has to learn what the *main thing* is. In driving, for example, the "main thing" is to keep the gas pedal pressed down. For Paul, the main thing was to make sure he taught people the truth about the Gospel. Paul willingly went and talked to the apostles at Jerusalem so there would be no misunderstanding about what he had been teaching. The apostles agreed with Paul's teaching and commended him for his faithfulness.

A lot of times we can become more concerned with things that are part of Christianity but aren't the main thing. Have you ever noticed that unsaved people often think Christianity is all about *not* doing certain things? We're giving them that impression! What can you do today to make Christ the main thing—both for your own growth and for other people to see?

THURSDAY • Galatians 2:7-14

DIGGING DEEPER There are ways we can tell who is on the same team in a soccer game. Players wearing the same color is a good clue. Another hint is when the ball is kicked into the goal and the players from that team create a body pile in the middle of the field, with their teammate on the bottom. Paul had the same reason for preaching the Gospel as did Peter, James, and John. The only difference was to whom they preached. Paul had been sent by God to the Gentiles while Peter, James, and John were sent to the Jews. Each of them had the same purpose, power, and call from God. They were just going different places.

Are there specific people you think God wants you to share the Gospel with? Look around for people who may not be being reached.

FRIDAY • Galatians 2:15-21

DIGGING DEEPER In today's passage, Paul reminds the Galatians that justification and righteousness do not come from keeping the Old Testament Law, which was given to the Jews. Rather, they come only through belief in Jesus Christ, which was the truth Paul taught. When someone was found guilty in court during Paul's day, he could be declared righteous by the judge only after he had worked off the debt of his offense. But our debt as sinners is impossible to work off because it requires that we make a perfect sacrifice, which we cannot do. Christ does all the debt-paying for us (v. 20).

Christ doesn't just take care of our debt—He keeps working after salvation (v. 20). Do you ever struggle with still trying to "keep the law" to please God, when it should be Christ living through you?

SATURDAY • Galatians 3:1-9

DIGGING DEEPER In a court of law, each side presents evidence in order to persuade the jury to its way of thinking. The outcome depends on which side presents the best evidence, in the best way, and convinces the jury. With this thought in mind, Paul asks the Galatians if they are truly so foolish as to think they could earn their salvation by works of the Law, and then remain righteous by doing those same good works found in the Law. Paul is asking them what evidence they have that would support such a conclusion. Paul reminds the believers that Abraham's righteousness was the result of his faith in God, not his works, and that it is because of Abraham's faith, we now have a chance at the same works-less faith (v. 8).

Do you do good works because you have faith, or are you doing those works to get salvation or to try to please God?

WEEK 11

No one likes the idea of being put in prison and losing his freedom. This week we will learn that the value of the Law in the Old Testament was to teach us the freedom we have in Christ. Those who continue to live by the Law forfeit the freedom they have in Christ, choosing bondage.

PRAYER FOCUS FOR THIS WEEK

THE QUESTION: What is the writer saying?

THE ANSWER: How can I apply this to my life?

SUNDAY • Galatians 3:10-16

DIGGING DEEPER When a criminal is convicted, punishment follows. The sentence may be death or prison time, but there are always consequences. The "curse" of the Law in today's passage signifies being handed over to the judgment and wrath of God. This is a serious thing, and the word *under* (v. 10) means that rather than merely facing the possibility of a future punishment, the follower of the Law is already subject to the wrath of God. The good news, however, is that Christ has redeemed us from the curse, and we can be free from that wrath. Christ bought our freedom.

God's judgment is already here, but so is His salvation. Who do you know today whom you should tell about the freedom of Christ?

MONDAY • Galatians 3:17-22

DIGGING DEEPER Promises, promises, promises! We hear them from everyone, but not many are kept. The word promise in Scripture means "a notification of agreement" or "to announce an intention." Paul focuses on God's promise to Abraham from the Old Testament when He said, "In thee shall all nations of the earth be blessed" (Genesis 12:3). The promise God referred to in Genesis would be fulfilled in the future death and resurrection of Christ, Who provided salvation for all. God always keeps His promises!

Name a promise to you that God has kept. What is a promise you have made to God? Have you kept it? Is there something you need to do to make it right, so that you keep a promise you've made either to God or others?

TUESDAY • Galatians 3:23-29

DIGGING DEEPER It is not uncommon to have a tutor help us with a certain subject or give us a better understanding of a topic. Paul refers to the Law as a schoolmaster or tutor that teaches us about Christ and our need for salvation. The Old Testament taught the people about God's righteous requirement, which they could not meet. Not being able to live by His standards pushed them toward faith in God, and faith in how He would eventually provide salvation. The Law, even today, teaches us that we can't do it on our own. We need to trust in God and His righteousness.

One way to really understand and appreciate God's righteousness and salvation is to work as hard as you can and see if you can be a truly good person on your own. Try it for a day! You will quickly see how far we are from keeping God's standard. This humility helps us put true faith in God.

WEDNESDAY • Galatians 4:1-7

DIGGING DEEPER When it comes to privileges and authority, there are days when it seems that teenagers are at the bottom of the food chain. The only ones they have authority over are younger siblings and the dog. But one day that control is lifted, and they find themselves with greater privileges and freedoms because they are adults. Life in Christ means that we are sons of God because of God's love. Children have all the privileges of being part of a family, and it is the same when we are part of God's family. A son in the New Testament was given a signet ring with the family symbol on it, which gave him the same authority as his father. The Holy Spirit (v. 6) is our signet ring from God.

List two privileges and responsibilities from Scripture we have as children of God. What privilege or responsibility will you claim today?

THURSDAY • Galatians 4:8-18

DIGGING DEEPER When you learn to drive, there is a ton of stuff to remember. There are things you're supposed to do, things you are not supposed to do, and you have to remember it within a moment's notice. In today's passage, Paul reminded the Gentiles in Galatia of the basics of being a Christian: 1) Don't be in bondage to idols, or demons, or other men (v. 8); 2) know God and serve Him (v. 9); 3) don't turn to earthly methods of doing good that are weak and do not really work (v. 9b); 4) Return to doing what is good, and be passionate about it (v. 18).

What Paul is writing about here is one of the hardest parts of the Christian life. Understanding salvation is great the first time, but remembering that truth—and living like we know it—is where the real battle is. Do you ever fall back into good works? What can you do to change that today?

FRIDAY • Galatians 4:19-26

DIGGING DEEPER Have you ever tried to give advice or make a suggestion, and someone responded with "You're not my boss!" or "Who died and left you in charge?" Too often, we want to run our own lives according to our own plans, and we see help from others as interference. Paul is asking the Christians in Galatia why they are not satisfied with God's promises. They instead were seeking after the inferior teachings of men. He uses the illustration of Abraham, who would not wait for God to fulfill His promise of giving him a child (Isaac). Instead, he had a child through another woman, hoping that would be okay. Abraham created a mess because he would not trust God, and the Galatians were doing the same.

Name an area of your life, such as friends or free time, in which you have taken control from God. Pray and take the right steps to give it back to Him.

SATURDAY • Galatians 4:27-5:1

DIGGING DEEPER Paul is building on his contrast between *freedom* and *bondage*. Just as Isaac was the "child of promise" to Abraham and Sarah, so those who trust in Christ by faith are also "children of promise." As such, all (v. 26) people of faith are free a) from bondage to paganism (4:8), b) from bondage to Jewish legalism (4:5), and c) from any other teaching that seeks to draw those of faith back under the yoke of works (5:1) to earn salvation. Have you ever heard the saying "He who is a slave to the compass has the freedom of the seas"? A sailor with compass in hand has freedom to travel the globe, but without that compass he is just lost. A slave to God's promises has freedom from sin's bondage.

Sin may seem like more fun, but we need to ask God to help us see how it can entrap us. What areas of bondage do you need to get rid of today?

WEEK 12

It's one thing when someone accomplishes something, but isn't it better when a team achieves together, and everyone can celebrate? This week we learn that believers in the Spirit serve God best when we do it together.

PRAYER FOCUS FOR THIS WEEK

THE QUESTION: What is the writer saying?

THE ANSWER: How can I apply this to my life?

SUNDAY • Galatians 5:2-6

DIGGING DEEPER Paul reminds the church that even though circumcision, or the Law, was good because it identified the Jewish people as God's chosen ones, it was not more important than faith in Christ. The Jewish Law was given by God at a time in history when He wanted to direct His people toward righteousness and remind them that their salvation was not in keeping the Law, but through faith in His forgiveness. The true basis for salvation is found in verse 5: (a) through the Spirit, (b) by faith, and (c) in the hope of righteousness. No personal works are mixed in—it's only through faith in Christ.

As good as our human efforts may be in our Christian walk, they're nothing compared to what God can do through us. How can you adjust your focus to be on Christ today?

MONDAY • Galatians 5:7-15

DIGGING DEEPER Have you ever seen someone in the Olympics or at a track meet run into another runner, tripping him, and knocking him off course? That is the picture Paul paints when he asks, "Who hindered you from obeying the truth?" The false teachers had tried to trip the Galatians up in their understanding of God's Word, and Paul was bringing that to their attention. Like every good coach, Paul reminded them of their past success and of his confidence that they would again succeed. In order to "run well" they were to (a) serve one another (v. 13), (b) love their neighbors (v. 14), (c) take heed of their conduct (v. 15), (d) walk (v. 16) and live (v. 25) in the Spirit, and (e) desire humility (v. 26).

Can you think of a time when you were tripped up in pursuit of the truth? What can you do to avoid falling today?

TUESDAY • Galatians 5:16-21

DIGGING DEEPER Have you ever seen a video game where the cars can go off the road and slam into buildings or knock over fire hydrants, causing big crashes? It's not like that in real life. We have boundaries in which we need to drive. The same is true of our spiritual walk. We can walk in the Spirit by staying within the guidelines of Scripture, or we can walk in our flesh and allow our sinful nature to control our actions and attitudes. Today's passage includes a lengthy list of guidelines that tip us off to certain behaviors that involve no good. Some are pretty obvious, but others you may not be as familiar with. Grab a commentary or another Bible translation if you need to so you can see why Paul picks each different area—we need to be wary of them all!

Which of these areas need attention in your life?

WEDNESDAY • Galatians 5:22-26

DIGGING DEEPER Remember when you had an opportunity to pick fruit from a tree, or strawberries off the plant? It was no surprise that you found apples on a tree or berries on the plant! Good, healthy trees and plants produce the fruit after their kind. Imagine how peculiar (and dangerous) it would be if watermelons grew on trees! Today's passage is a reminder that the evidence of what is going on in our hearts and minds is the *fruit* we produce. When we read the list in today's passage, we understand that our lives are to reflect Christ and what He has to offer. These characteristics show God's glory as we serve others.
Which fruit of the Spirit do you think shows up most in your life? Which do you struggle with? Ask God for His guidance as He helps you grow toward producing all types of fruit.

THURSDAY • Galatians 6:1-5

DIGGING DEEPER Paul tells us that we are responsible to help those who are "being overtaken in a fault" (v. 1). Overtaken means "drawn into a trap and taken." It is coupled with fault ("to misplace one's step; to slip and fall"). Thus, Paul gives a picture of a brother who falls into the mud of sin because he is careless, not having considered the steps that led him into the trap. A spirit-filled Christian (one being led by the Spirit and is growing) shouldn't say, "Well, it's his own fault, let him suffer! Maybe next time he will be more careful." We all struggle with different sins and easily slip in the mud or fall in traps. Love demands that the spirit-filled believer come to the aid of the overtaken and help restore him.
Why is it so hard for us, when someone sins, to restore fellow Christians? Why should we help in any way we can?

FRIDAY • Galatians 6:6-10

DIGGING DEEPER It is always good to know the rules, because then we can prepare. If you get caught driving without your seatbelt, the rule is that you will get a ticket. If you plant watermelon seeds, you will get watermelons. Again, today we learn a biblical life principle illustrated by a common occurrence. When we set our hearts, minds, and wills on being a servant of our flesh, we will reap corruption. Paul once again encourages his readers by reminding them that if they do not get tired of doing good deeds, they will reap good fruit instead of works of the flesh. The best way to fight the good fight is with the help of others (v. 10).

We know the rules of life, and we know what God says are danger areas (5:19-21) and good fruits (5:22-23). How can you help another believer focus on pursuing right today? How can you do good to others (v. 10)?

SATURDAY • Galatians 6:11-18

DIGGING DEEPER To stress importance, Paul takes the pen from his scribe and writes this last paragraph with bold letters. The three sections of the conclusion correspond, in reverse order, to the three sections of the letter. First, he warns that the false teachers, who were telling (v. 12) the Galatians to be circumcised, were not interested in their spiritual welfare. Second, Paul makes a final defense of his own credentials. Third, he says he has marks (v. 17) on his body to prove his arguments are true. Paul loved his brothers in Christ. This was what motivated him to reprove, encourage, and instruct them about their walks with Christ.

Paul's final assault on poor teaching is also a reminder that the faithful Christian walk can be lived—he did it! He ends by pointing to Christ. What lesson from this week do you want Christ to teach you more about today?

WEEK 13

Staying strong for God is an area where every believer struggles. The story of Daniel is encouraging because he settled Who he would worship and obey before he was tested, and the results were amazing. Learn how to follow God in an ungodly world by watching Daniel over the next couple weeks.

PRAYER FOCUS FOR THIS WEEK

THE QUESTION: What is the writer saying?

THE ANSWER: How can I apply this to my life?

SUNDAY • Daniel 1:1-8

DIGGING DEEPER Could you imagine what it would be like to live in total poverty and under constant threat of war? How would you respond if that enemy captured you but instead of killing and torturing you, placed you in a beautiful palace, gave you the best food, and literally treated you like royalty? Would you being thankful agree to do what they asked—even worship their gods? What if the penalty was death if you didn't? These were the conditions Daniel faced. Verse 8 says though that his response was to not give in. How about you? If you are a believer you do live in enemy territory—planet earth. There is pressure to conform to the world's standards. It's tempting to compromise. Will you dare to be a Daniel?
What areas of life tempt you to compromise your faith in God? How can you fight it? Are you using every available source… including God's help?

MONDAY • Daniel 1:9-21

DIGGING DEEPER Are you one to follow the crowd even when what those people are doing is wrong? Do your friends influence you more than you influence them? Do you set trends or follow them? How you answer these questions reveals how you respond to peer pressure. Daniel was able to resist giving in to this pressure because his heart's desire was to please God more than others. As a result his actions encouraged others to join him in obeying God (vv. 11-12). God then blessed them and used their example to influence even more people (vv. 15-16). If you are willing to take a stand for God, God will bless you and others will be influenced positively!

Think about the last time you gave in to negative peer pressure. What did it say about your heart's desire? Is pleasing God more important to you than pleasing others? What should you change to be like Daniel?

TUESDAY • Daniel 2:1-13

DIGGING DEEPER Have you ever had a nightmare that woke you from a sound sleep then kept you awake? It may have been so bizarre that it didn't make any sense. You may even have gone looking for help figuring out what it meant. Real life sometimes can be just as bizarre and you need help understanding how it all makes sense. So where do you go for help? Believers know that the answers to life's questions are found in the person of Jesus Christ and His Word, the Bible. Check out Psalm 119:9-11. If you want to know the answers look in the Book!

Can you think of any friends who need help understanding life from God's perspective? How can you be prepared to help them? How can Bible study help you?

WEDNESDAY • Daniel 2:14-23

DIGGING DEEPER Daniel and his friends understood one thing about God: Regardless of how unfair or out-of-control life may sometimes be, God is *always* in control! They knew that nothing was impossible for God—not even a complex dream (v. 22). Instead of running from his killers Daniel confronts them and asks for time. Instead of worrying he and his friends prayed to the One Who was in control. It wasn't until they prayed that the answer they needed was revealed. How often do we resort to prayer as our last option to life's problems when it should be the first thing we do? **How would your response to the problems you face be different if you followed Daniel's example and prayed? How can knowing that God is in control help you through difficult trials?**

THURSDAY • Daniel 2:24-30

DIGGING DEEPER Have you ever taken credit for something you didn't do? Maybe you had a school project that your parents did most of the work on but you got the good grade. You gladly accepted the grade but deep inside you knew you didn't deserve the recognition. In today's passage Daniel could have taken credit for interpreting the king's dream but he was wise enough not to try to steal God's glory. The king needed to understand that God was in control! God gives every believer gifts and abilities. We are to do exactly what Daniel did: Give all the glory to God! **Can you name a gift or talent that God has given you? Do you accept personal praise from others or give God all the glory for it? God often gives us these gifts as a way to show Himself to other people. How can you bring more glory to God in your life?**

FRIDAY • Daniel 2:31-43

DIGGING DEEPER What did the king eat before he went to bed? Whatever it was stay away from it! Actually God was giving the king a glimpse into the future of the world. The king needed to see the bigger picture and understand that life was not all about him. He needed to know that any power he had as the ruler of an empire was limited (v. 39 "after you shall arise"). It was a result of God's grace and part of His plan (vv. 37-38). We will probably never have such a dream but we have something much better. God's Word says exactly what will happen here on earth and Who is ultimately in control.

Do you sometimes act like you are the center of the universe? Think about your attitude in everyday life or how you treat others. What do these verses teach you about Who is really in control?

SATURDAY • Daniel 2:44-49

DIGGING DEEPER Did you notice the closing verses of chapter 2? Compare verse 13 with verse 46. What caused the change in the king's attitude? He recognized God's position of authority and power. Instead of killing Daniel the king promoted him to a national ruler. Daniel and his friends were rewarded with positions of authority and influence because of their faithfulness to God and His commandments (v. 49). Daniel trusted God to work and He did. We can expect God to do the same for us when we are faithful. Taking a stand for God, especially in front of those in authority can be scary. But if you honor God like Daniel did He will honor you.

Can people in authority in your life trust you like the king trusted Daniel? Do you and your friends have a reputation of being godly? If not what needs to change?

WEEK 14

Friends are a major influence in people's lives. Having friends that have the same goals encourages you to stand strong in tough times. This week we'll look at what makes good friends. Use what you learn to help you choose your friends.

PRAYER FOCUS FOR THIS WEEK

THE QUESTION: What is the writer saying?

THE ANSWER: How can I apply this to my life?

SUNDAY • Daniel 3:1-7

DIGGING DEEPER "Everybody's doing it!" You've probably heard this at school when people talk about drugs, drinking, sex, or cheating on tests. Even though there are Biblical principles for each of these areas most people would rather follow culture's standard of what's right and wrong. You probably face a constant barrage of choices between obeying God's Word or what your friends say. Today's passage stresses the real question you are answering when you make life choices: "Who are you going to worship—God or man?" Or to put it another way, "Who do you want to please—God or man?" Here's a hint: The popular choice almost always pleases man.

Are you living to please God? How is that being reflected in the choices you are making?

MONDAY • Daniel 3:8-18

DIGGING DEEPER We usually admire confidence in other people. Don't you like to be around confident people? Their attitude rubs off on you. What do you think makes them confident? Usually they know what they believe and why they believe it and they never waver. Their beliefs acted as a compass helping them navigate through their decisions. In these verses the confidence of Shadrach, Meshach, and Abednego astounded even the king. When faced with death these three were sure of three things (v. 17): 1) "our God"—they knew and believed in the Lord personally, 2) "is able to deliver"—they had experienced His deliverance before (chapter 2), and 3) they would not waver (vv. 16, 18).
Where is your confidence? Do you feel like with God you never have to waver? Why or why not? Do others see this confidence in you?

TUESDAY • Daniel 3:19-30

DIGGING DEEPER Making the decision to follow God wholeheartedly is not just a one-time thing. Every day you will be pressured to decide who you will worship. Your actions show who you're really trusting. Verse 28 says that these guys yielded their bodies, meaning they made choices that showed who they were following. Are you determined to worship God even if it costs personal comfort? God is looking for people who will not bow to the idols of today's world. How can you make sure you are not using your body to worship the idols of today? Can you think of specific areas where you may be tempted or struggling?
Are your friends determined to worship God with their bodies? If so commit to pray and meet for encouragement and accountability. If not, ask God to help you find some friends who are.

DIGGING DEEPER Where do your friends turn for help when they are in trouble? When they are looking for answers to difficult problems who do they go to? Are you at the top of their list? Can your friends count on you to give them godly advice even if it hurts? Daniel's reputation as God's man (vv. 8, 9, 18) was well respected. He was sought after. Chances are many of your friends are trying to make sense out of life. They are looking for answers and truth. If you are a follower of Christ you know that Jesus is the answer. Have you shared what you know with them? Do they know they can come to you to learn about God? Do you have the reputation of being God's representative?

Have you been faithfully sharing the Gospel with your friends? How are you preparing yourself to be ready to help others when they ask?

THURSDAY • Daniel 4:19-27

DIGGING DEEPER Do you think it would be cool to be able to know what will happen in the future? Daniel had been given the ability and the responsibility to share what he knew with the king but it didn't excite him because the news wasn't very good. His message was one of judgment on the king. Yet while it would be harsh (v. 25) it was not without hope. Repentance could save the king from being judged (v. 27). In a similar way, we have been given the ability to know according to God's Word the future of sinful men (Romans 6:23a). While it seems harsh, it is certainly not without hope (Romans 6:23b). We have the responsibility to share the Gospel with people (Matthew 28:19-20) and to encourage them to repent.

Are you willing to take your responsibility seriously when it comes to sharing the Gospel with your friends? Which friends need to hear?

FRIDAY • Daniel 4:28-37

DIGGING DEEPER How do you respond when someone gives you advice? What's your gut reaction? How do you deal with warnings from others? Someone who ignores warnings or doesn't listen to advice has a prideful attitude, something God hates. He sometimes has to bring humbling or humiliating experiences into life to teach us that we are not as great as we think we are. Nebuchadnezzar had to learn this lesson the hard way; but at least he learned it! He responded in a way that brought God glory. Every ability and talent you have is because God by His grace chose to give it to you. We need to learn how to continually give that glory back to God rather than have an attitude like Nebuchadnezzar's.

Ask someone who knows you to identify any prideful attitudes in your life. What do you need to do to change?

SATURDAY • Daniel 5:1-16

DIGGING DEEPER How is your reputation? What do you think your friends at school say about you when you're not around? Do people look to you for godly advice or the latest gossip? Do friends expect you to cause trouble or help them to get out of tough situations? The king in today's passage knew he was in serious trouble but even after asking everyone he knew for answers he was clueless! Daniel was his last and best hope for answers because his reputation was that of a person who had God's Spirit. No one questioned Who he believed and served. Although the king had never met Daniel, he "had heard" all about him (vv. 14, 16) and trusted him.

Ask your closest friends to help you evaluate your reputation. Does it reflect the character traits found in verses 11-12? How should you change?

WEEK 15

What do you do when life seems out of control? Someone has said that the true measure of a person is not how they respond when things are going well but rather what they do when their world is shaken. This week watch Daniel's response in hard times and discover his secret for staying steadfast.

PRAYER FOCUS FOR THIS WEEK

THE QUESTION: What is the writer saying?
THE ANSWER: How can I apply this to my life?

SUNDAY • Daniel 5:17-31

DIGGING DEEPER Have you ever been confronted by a parent or teacher about a sinful attitude? How did you respond? Were you arrogant, refusing to admit your guilt, or did you humbly ask forgiveness from the person you offended? Imagine if the person you offended was God Himself. What if He personally confronted you? Arrogance and pride are attitudes God hates and judges. Had the king been humble and repented of these attitudes perhaps the story would have ended differently, but there is no indication he did. Pride destroyed this king—don't let it destroy you! **Prideful attitudes are often behind other sins we struggle with whether we know it or not. Think hard about the way you see yourself and the way you see God. How have your actions this week been affected by those views? Are you willing to repent and ask God for forgiveness?**

MONDAY • Daniel 6:1-15

DIGGING DEEPER Trying to live in a way that pleases God can make you many enemies. Christians are often a target for harassment and sometimes even death. Cassie Bernall was a Christian teen in Littleton, Colorado who had decided to live her life in a way that pleased God. When some of her classmates attacked the school in a shooting rampage they singled out Cassie and asked her if she followed God. She said "yes," knowing it would cost her life. Like Daniel, possible consequences did not keep her from following God.

How would you respond if you were in the same situation as Cassie or Daniel? Would the threat of death keep you from following God? Are you maintaining a faithful testimony for Christ today? How does it show?

TUESDAY • Daniel 6:16-28

DIGGING DEEPER Believing in God does not mean you will never face hard times. In fact a lot of situations may be tougher because of your faith in Him. Isn't it good to know that no matter what, He is with you? These problems and trials are even a way to show those around you that you are trusting God. Nothing in this passage suggests that Daniel complained about his treatment. The king however noticed his behavior. In verses 16 and 20 it says the king saw that Daniel "served God continually." Daniel understood God was in control (v. 22) so he trusted His wisdom and refused to complain.

What trial are you facing in your life today? Have you been complaining? Do you understand that God is in control? What should your attitude be? Even something as small as not complaining can be a great testimony.

WEDNESDAY • Daniel 7:1-14

DIGGING DEEPER In case you forgot Who's in control here's another reminder. In yesterday's passage Daniel learned that God takes care of individuals. But what about worldwide problems? Can God really be in control of everything at all times? Today's verses shout a very loud "YES!" Through Daniel's visions we get a glimpse of world history from God's perspective. God is still on the throne even as various human governments come and go. Whether in the best of times or in the worst of times He is still ruling over world events! Presidents and kings will come and go but God's kingdom will never end (v. 14). Knowing this helps us trust Him with everyday circumstances.

What areas of life are you worried about? What can you do to remind yourself of how God is in control?

THURSDAY • Daniel 7:15-28

DIGGING DEEPER What is the worst storm you've experienced? Can you remember the sickening feeling you had as you saw it coming or watched it destroy what was in its path? Daniel had the same feeling but knew that something much worse than a storm was coming in the future. What kinds of emotions and reactions did Daniel experience (vv. 15, 28)? The news definitely changed his outlook and how he thought about things. He was troubled not only because of the earthly destruction but also because that destruction included people. With these events possibly happening in our lifetime, we should have a similar response.

How do God's plans or warnings for the future affect your outlook? Are you concerned for people? What do you need to do to change today after hearing this news?

DIGGING DEEPER Do you realize that the next event on God's timeline is the Rapture of the Church? Christians will suddenly be caught up to meet Christ in the air without warning. Most of the prophetic writings recorded in Scripture were written hundreds of years before they were fulfilled, yet time and again God has kept these promises. Throughout history God has warned men and showed them the way of escape; yet many still ignore Him or don't believe His teaching. It's our job to keep spreading the word. You can trust the Bible to be true.

Learning about which prophecies have been fulfilled is a great way to strengthen your faith and prepare you to talk to others. Talk to a youth leader or do some research today.

SATURDAY • Daniel 8:15-27

DIGGING DEEPER Have you ever been confused to the point of frustration? Imagine how Daniel felt trying to understand the meaning of all the incredible visions—beasts in every shape and size, angels, judgments, etc. God did not leave him confused. He sent the angel Gabriel to explain the visions. Are there things in the Bible that confuse you? What about things happening in your life today that don't make sense? Don't give up—look up! If you ask God in faith for the wisdom to understand His perspective on your problem He will answer you (James 1:5).

What are some areas that are causing you frustration? Do you have confidence that God is in control? Have you asked Him to help you see His perspective? How can you demonstrate real faith as you deal with it?

WEEK 16

This week, Daniel is going to learn some incredible things about what the last days are going to be like. God's awesomeness left Daniel speechless! When you read about what he saw you might be left speechless too.

PRAYER FOCUS FOR THIS WEEK

THE QUESTION: What is the writer saying?

THE ANSWER: How can I apply this to my life?

SUNDAY • Daniel 9:1-10

DIGGING DEEPER It's easy to point fingers at the team member who caused the team to lose—the one who fumbled the ball or struck out in the final play. The truth is that your team probably lost because of a series of errors during the entire game. Each member must take responsibility. Daniel, being a righteous man could have been bitter about having to endure captivity in Babylon. He could point fingers at his fellow countrymen for their sins. Instead he looked in the mirror of God's Word (v. 2), took personal responsibility for his situation before God, and repented (v. 4). He admitted his sin, attitudes, actions (vv. 5-6), humbled himself (vv. 7-8), and appealed to God's character and faithfulness (v. 10).
How do you deal with sin in your life? Do you follow the pattern of repentance that Daniel set? Start doing it today!

MONDAY • Daniel 9:11-19

DIGGING DEEPER Getting what you deserve is justice. A killer getting serious jail time is one example of justice. When your brother or sister gets punished for doing wrong that's justice too. But it feels different when you get it, right? Even when you deserve justice you probably fight it. It goes back to the pride and selfishness we all have. Pride is a serious sin in God's eyes. It is at the root of all the trouble we have obeying and trusting Him. Pride is often the cause when people don't submit to authority, are unwilling to listen to others, have an unteachable spirit, are not willing to change, or are boastful. These attitudes got Israel into captivity. Only full repentance—changing minds about sinful pride and doing things God's way—can fix it. It took Israel 70 years to repent.
How are your sinful attitudes like Israel's? When will you repent?

TUESDAY • Daniel 9:20-27

DIGGING DEEPER Have you ever experienced times when your fellowship with God just wasn't right? Perhaps you've felt distant like He wasn't close. Have you considered that sin in your life could be a reason for it? Sin keeps you from being in fellowship with God. But if you live with a continual attitude of repentance (confessing and turning from sin as you commit it) and obedience you will not feel far from God. In today's passage we see that Daniel's willingness to humble himself, pray, and confess his sin (v. 20) resulted in God's swift response (v. 21). He also learned some incredible things from God (vv. 24-27).
How would you rate your relationship with the Lord? Do you feel close to God? How much do you obey or trust Him? What can you change to make your walk more consistent?

WEDNESDAY • Daniel 10:1-9

DIGGING DEEPER What does it take for you to get excited about God? Throughout the entire book Daniel never takes God's awesome presence, protection, or power for granted. Because He had a heart that was sensitive to and sought to please God, he had witnessed God working in incredible ways! He got to see things no one else did (v. 7). Because he pursued holiness he received understanding from God. He even saw the Lord (vv. 5-6)! While we may never have the visions that Daniel had we still must pursue holiness if we want to see God (Hebrews 12:14). **Ask your youth leaders what pursuing holiness means to them. What do they do to become what God calls "holy"? How can you begin your own pursuit of holiness?**

THURSDAY • Daniel 10:10-21

DIGGING DEEPER Part of using computers today is having antivirus or firewall protection because there are people out there who spend their time trying to hack into computers and steal personal information, passwords, or money. In the same way Satan has his spiritual hackers (demons) who try to influence the lives of believers and even nations. God's firewall (angels) do battle on our behalf (Hebrews 1:14). Sometimes the battles are long (v. 13) but you must never give up praying and seeking God. He will strengthen you (v. 16). **Praying with another person can help you remain strong and faithful. Who can you ask to pray with today? What specific things can you pray for that you found in today's lesson?**

FRIDAY • Daniel 11:36-12:2

DIGGING DEEPER Have you ever really disliked a character in a movie or a play that keeps causing trouble for others? It seems like he keeps getting away with what he's doing but just when you think he's escaped, judgment arrives. Who hasn't cheered when this happens? In today's passage this king (the Antichrist) is pictured as one causing serious trouble but he is finally judged at the time God intended. Notice his attitudes in verses 36-37. Think about yourself—do you do any of these things? Are you extremely self-willed (rebellious to authority), self-centered (want your own way), self-worshiping (me first!), foul-mouthed, a God-hater, a lover of war and destruction (like violence too much), or a lover of money (greedy)?
Are any of these traits evident in your life? There is no room for any of these things in the life of a child of God. Get rid of them!

SATURDAY • Daniel 12:4-13

DIGGING DEEPER Learning and studying about the last days is very exciting! It can also be frustrating because some parts are just too difficult to understand. Today we can see how certain prophecies are being fulfilled; but there are others that still baffle us. God wants us to study what He says but He also wants us to balance this with our other responsibilities; such as sharing the Gospel, making disciples, and living a holy life. Christ may or may not return in your lifetime and that's OK. If you know Christ as your Savior "You shall rest and will arise to your inheritance at the end of the days" (v. 13).
How are you doing in fulfilling your responsibilities? Which one is a struggle for you? Talk to a believer you look up to about how to work on this part of the Christian life.

WEEK 17

Peter will always be known by the church as a man of action. In this letter, you'll see why he earned his reputation as he attacks the false teachers of his day head-on. He is confident God will triumph in the end.

PRAYER FOCUS FOR THIS WEEK

THE QUESTION: What is the writer saying?

THE ANSWER: How can I apply this to my life?

SUNDAY • 2 Peter 1:1-4

DIGGING DEEPER What do you think of when you see or hear the word *powerful*? You may think of the center of our solar system, the sun. Others might think of Niagara Falls or the whitewater rapids your youth group recently tried to conquer. Maybe electricity seems powerful to you. But how many of us think about Jesus? We don't often describe Him as powerful. Peter lets us know that not only is Jesus powerful but He also makes His power available to us as we pursue a holy life. Have you accessed His power today? Don't try to live the Christian life in your own strength. Let our *powerful* Savior help you.

Jesus has power even in the hard-to-change parts of our spiritual lives. How can you remind yourself throughout today that He is powerful and wants to help you?

MONDAY • 2 Peter 1:5-9

DIGGING DEEPER God expects you to live a certain kind of life! In these verses Peter makes a list of various qualities and characteristics that believers should consider *normal* for their everyday walk. First on the list is *virtue* (v. 5) which is simply moral excellence. God expects us to have lives where we do what's right. *Knowledge* (v. 5) comes next and implies that the Christian should study God's Word. *Temperance* (v. 6) follows knowledge. It's a fancy word for self-control. Next is *patience* (v. 6) or perseverance which is the ability to continue doing right no matter what circumstances we're in. *Godliness* (v. 6) is doing what God says with reverence to Who He is. And *brotherly kindness* (v. 7) is more than just being nice. It is sacrificing for each other.
How are you doing? Which qualities do you need to work on most?

TUESDAY • 2 Peter 1:10-14

DIGGING DEEPER Repetition is the key to learning. Repetition is the key to learning. Repetition is the key to learning. Do you get the point? When teachers repeat something what are they trying to do? They want to make sure you really understand what they're saying. If they continue to repeat something over and over again they want you never to forget it. Peter admits that he's been trying to do this. Essentially he says, "I am going to keep reminding you of the importance of showing virtue, knowledge, and these other qualities in your lives even though you already know about them and are putting them into practice." Peter says, "Get it and never forget it!"
Do you get it? How often do you need to be reminded? What two qualities or characteristics will you work on this week?

WEDNESDAY • 2 Peter 1:15-21

DIGGING DEEPER   Has anybody ever accused you of believing in fairy tales and fables because you're a Christian? It happens to a lot of us. It has been happening to Christians since the days of the disciples. In fact Peter is addressing this when he says, "We have not followed cunningly devised fables" (v. 16) but we were rather "eyewitnesses of His majesty." In a nutshell Peter says, "We're not making this resurrection thing up. We actually saw Jesus!" History tells us that all these eyewitnesses were so sure they saw Jesus alive that they were willing to die for that belief. Would you die for a fairy tale?
How would you respond to someone who said the Bible was a bunch of stories and fairy tales? What would you be willing to die for?

THURSDAY • 2 Peter 2:1-9

DIGGING DEEPER   Have you ever seen professional impersonators? It is amazing how well they can imitate famous people like presidents or Elvis. An impersonator is someone who looks and sounds the same on the outside but in reality is completely different. In our passage today Peter warns of those who impersonate him and others who share the good news. He calls them "false prophets" and "false teachers" and warns us to watch out for their destructive words. They bring doom.
How can you know if someone who claims to be a "Bible teacher" is an impersonator ("false teacher") or not? What will you do if you encounter someone who isn't the real thing?

DIGGING DEEPER If you were asked to describe what your best friend looked like what kind of words would you use? You would try to be specific so that if people saw him on the street they could recognize him. This is exactly what Peter does for us as he describes false prophets and teachers. He wants us to know them when we see them. He tells us they are *presumptuous* (v. 10) which would indicate arrogance in assuming they know the truth, and *self-willed* (v. 10) which would tell us they might be stubborn. He goes into great detail about how wicked they are accusing them of having "eyes full of adultery" (v. 14) and summing it up by saying they have "forsaken the right way" (v. 15). Now you know what to look for!

How would others describe your spiritual life? What kind of adjectives would they use?

SATURDAY • 2 Peter 2:17-22

DIGGING DEEPER Have you ever been around people who talked and talked—and talked some more? And on top of that they never really said anything? You may have someone in mind. Well, this is the description given of false teachers in this section of Scripture. Specifically Peter says, "they speak great swelling words of vanity" (v. 18) which means they talk a lot using big words and catchy phrases but ultimately say nothing at all. How disappointing it is to hear lots of words but learn nothing at all. People should not only say something; they should have something to say especially when they present themselves as having truth and the way to life and knowing God.

Do you know people like this? How should you respond to their teaching? What should you do when it comes to your own words?

WEEK 18

There will always be those who oppose Christianity and do their best to change its message. Peter and Jude both understand that. They warn us to avoid the ways of these scoffers and to defend our faith.

PRAYER FOCUS FOR THIS WEEK

THE QUESTION: What is the writer saying?

THE ANSWER: How can I apply this to my life?

SUNDAY • 2 Peter 3:1-6

DIGGING DEEPER "I shall return." You may have run across that famous quote from General Douglas MacArthur in history class at one time. But do you know that Jesus said it first? Some 2,000 years ago Jesus promised that He would come back—He would return for His Church. Ever since He left though there have been people who challenged this truth. They say things like, "If He's coming then where is He?" or "What's taking Him so long?" just to stir up trouble. The fact is Jesus *is* coming back. He *will* return. It's not a matter of *if* but *when*. And when He returns He will come back not as a carpenter but as a conqueror!

If Jesus were to return for His Church tomorrow would you be ready? What would you like to be doing when Jesus returns?

MONDAY • 2 Peter 3:7-12

DIGGING DEEPER God loves people more than anything. That's a fact. He loves us so much that He's delaying Jesus' return so more people can respond to His love and have a relationship with Him. Specifically Peter says God's ultimate desire is that "all should come to repentance" (v. 9). Unfortunately not everyone responds positively to God's grace and love. Many people choose to reject His offer of abundant life on earth. When they do this they are also choosing to reject His offer of eternal life in Heaven. The choices we make today will affect us and others for eternity.

Pray for someone who needs to respond positively to God's invitation of eternal life. Now that you prayed can you do something about it?

TUESDAY • 2 Peter 3:13-18

DIGGING DEEPER When teaching from the Bible it's always good to conclude with some sort of action step. Everything God teaches us about Him and what He's done for us is intended to change our lives. As Peter finishes up his comments about those who try to distort Scripture he leaves his readers with one final instruction: "Grow in grace and in the knowledge of our Lord and Saviour Jesus Christ" (v. 18). Peter understands, as should we, that when we pursue spiritual maturity and a better relationship with Jesus we won't be led astray by false teachers like those he's been talking about throughout the book. He offers a warning to beware and a word of encouragement to grow.

Are you making progress in your spiritual life? Are you growing? What can you do today to develop a closer relationship with God?

WEDNESDAY • Jude 1-7

DIGGING DEEPER If you were having an important conversation with someone about something you really needed to talk about and a rat suddenly ran across the floor, would you stop your conversation? Of course you would! You'd take care of the new problem that was scampering right in front of you! That is what Jude does as he writes this letter. He wanted to write about one subject (salvation) but he saw a spiritual rat creeping in and wrote instead about the importance of defending the faith. Specifically he instructs believers to "earnestly contend for the faith" (v. 3). He said we need to take a stand against those who want to twist Scripture for their own personal purposes.

What are you doing to defend the faith? What can you do today? Does something else you've been working on need to be put aside?

THURSDAY • Jude 8-11

DIGGING DEEPER If the Bible were still being written today and God chose to comment on your life what kind of words would He use? We can't be sure of what He would say about us but we know what He said about three people—Cain, Balaam, and Korah. God's words were not in any way complimentary. In fact each of these men is associated with the most ungodly of men. We are told about them so we can avoid their serious mistakes. You can find Cain's rebellion in Genesis 4:1-15, Balaam's failures in Numbers 22-25, and Korah's ungodliness in Numbers 16:1-35. The end result of their evil choices is the same as anyone who chooses to go against God: divine judgment.

Do you have problem areas in your spiritual life that would be listed in a passage like this?

FRIDAY • Jude 12-19

DIGGING DEEPER Are you an empty rain cloud? How about a fruitless tree? Could you perhaps be a raging wave? Jude uses these phrases to describe the ungodly. He says they are clouds "without water" (v. 12), meaning they look like they're bringing helpful, cool water after a long drought but are actually empty. "Trees without fruit" (v. 12) is an instruction to pay attention to the results of these people's teaching—does spiritual growth happen or not? "Raging waves" (v. 13) means these people cause trouble for all they touch. The main point is this: The ungodly are dangerous, follow their selfishness, and do not know the true Spirit of God.
Could you be described as an empty rain cloud, fruitless tree, or raging wave? Do you give people God's solid truth?

SATURDAY • Jude 20-25

DIGGING DEEPER Are you good at building things? Some people are very skilled at making furniture, houses, bridges, or even skyscrapers. Whether or not you can build with your hands, you have a responsibility as a Christian to be building up your life (v. 20). 1 Corinthians 3:11 says that as believers we have a solid foundation. Jesus says in Matthew 7:24-27 that if we listen to and obey His teachings we will be "wise builders" as compared to unwise ones who don't think ahead or build on solid foundations. A well-constructed house or life is a beautiful sight and it is also very functional.
What kind of life are you building for yourself? Are you using the right foundation? Would God say it is both beautiful and functional?

WEEK 19

We all know we get in trouble when we don't do what's right. So life is easy, right? Just be perfect. But we know it's not that simple. Jeremiah has some tough challenges and the people he's talking to really have problems. But God helps clear things up this week when it comes to doing right and wrong.

PRAYER FOCUS FOR THIS WEEK

THE QUESTION: What is the writer saying?

THE ANSWER: How can I apply this to my life?

SUNDAY • Jeremiah 1:1-10

DIGGING DEEPER Verse 1 tells us Jeremiah was a priest. In verse 5 God calls him to be a prophet but Jeremiah wasn't quite interested in the job. Being a priest was a lot easier than being a prophet. A priest pretty much knew what to expect each day but a prophet spoke to a whole nation. God could send him anywhere and he sometimes had to be by himself. No wonder Jeremiah gave God a few excuses. His argument was that prophets do big things and he thought he wasn't cut out for it. In verses 8-10 God reassures him that He could protect, empower, and take care of anything that worried Jeremiah. God does the same for us. Nothing is too difficult!

Is there anything God wants you to do that you've been putting off? What worries do you have that God has promised to take care of?

MONDAY • Jeremiah 1:11-19

DIGGING DEEPER So what's the deal with almond branches and boiling pots? God often uses symbols to prove His point. Almond trees have flowers and the blooms are one of the first signs that spring is coming. God was telling Judah, "Get ready—something big is coming." Imagine someone pouring a huge pot of boiling water on you. Not fun! This is a symbol of God pouring punishment on Judah. The punishment would probably be an army from the north and it would attack Judah in the south. The key to remember in today's passage is verse 16. The people that lived in Jerusalem had punishment coming and Jeremiah had to be firm and tell them. Would this be scary? Yes. But verse 19 must have been great news.
Is there anything in your life that sounds too difficult right now? Do you believe God will protect you—no matter what?

TUESDAY • Jeremiah 2:1-13

DIGGING DEEPER Keep in mind that the message today was said to an entire city not just one person. The people of that city used to love God. God compared their relationship to a new marriage where they loved each other very much. The problem is that somebody broke the marriage—and it wasn't God. As time went on Jerusalem loved other false "gods." The main one was called Baal. Verse 13 sums it up: The people of Israel not only forgot Who loved them but they also thought they could find another fake god to do the same. As crazy as it seems sometimes we look for love in places other than God. We do the same thing.
Who or what do you talk about more than anything? Is it God? What things take the place of God in your life?

WEDNESDAY • Jeremiah 3:1-13

DIGGING DEEPER God's people lived in two territories during Jeremiah's day: Israel in the north and Judah with the city of Jerusalem in the south. Israel had already turned its back on God and now Jerusalem is doing the same. Jerusalem was so unfaithful that God calls the city a prostitute here. Then in verse 11 He says Israel was "more righteous" than Judah. This isn't because the Israelites were better but rather because they saw the punishment happen once already and they still left God. It's like a little brother or sister who saw an older sibling get in trouble but still made the same bad choices. The key word to remember today is "return"—that Judah was still in a place where it could turn to God.

When you sin how quick are you to return to God? What area of your life do you need to give up and "return" to God?

THURSDAY • Jeremiah 3:14-25

DIGGING DEEPER Ever been mad at one of your friends? It is a horrible feeling. You want to be friends but you won't stop being angry. Today we see that all the Lord God wanted was for His people to return to Him. Verses 14-20 are God describing all the good things He would do for those who returned. He didn't want to just dish out horrible punishment on them—He wanted to enjoy a love relationship! It's almost as if He's saying, "Isn't it so much better when we're friends?" Verses 22-25 says the people still had a chance to make things right but they didn't return to God. Even if they come back later punishment was still waiting. It's never worth it to stay away from God.

Do you ever wait to come back to God because you think it doesn't matter as long as you return eventually? What do today's verses say about this?

FRIDAY • Jeremiah 5:1-3, 12-19

DIGGING DEEPER Have you ever wanted something then realized later that it wasn't what you really wanted after all? That's where these people are today. They wanted something other than God. Jeremiah goes on a hunt (vv. 1-3). He's looking for just one person in the whole city that loves God. Not only can he not find one but the people call him a "wind bag" (vv. 13). God lovingly wants them to return but Jeremiah has to tell them the bad news (vv. 14-17)—that God will let them follow false gods but it will not be good for them in the end. The key is to enjoy God now and avoid the heartache later.

If you were in Jerusalem for Jeremiah's hunt for a person who loved God would he have found you? Is there anything you currently want more than your friendship with God?

SATURDAY • Jeremiah 5:20-31

DIGGING DEEPER In verse 22 God asks a tough question: Do we fear Him? Often we fear rejection from friends or embarrassment more than we fear God. But God is not just a powerful being Who can punish us—look at verse 25. It says that when we sin our actions cause good things to be withheld from us. God, being all-powerful and loving, points us in the right direction for our own good. The best way to see this loving God and the good things He brings is to know Him and to "fear" Him—to understand Who God is and let Him be in control of our lives. Fearing God brings good but ignoring Him leads to punishment and destruction.

Are you ever tempted to think you can control your life just as well as God could? Take a minute to think about some characteristics of God and ask God to help you understand Him and have a healthy fear of Him today.

WEEK 20

What if you could serve more than one god in your life? What if you could live two different lives—one at church and another where you could do anything you wanted to? Jeremiah promises that it's a rough life! Be thankful there's only one God and one way to live… for Him!

PRAYER FOCUS FOR THIS WEEK

THE QUESTION: What is the writer saying?

THE ANSWER: How can I apply this to my life?

SUNDAY • Jeremiah 6:10-20

DIGGING DEEPER Jeremiah knows punishment is coming but the people don't want to listen. Even the spiritual leaders are selfish and don't tell the truth. Verse 15 says they're not even ashamed to do wrong. The priests and prophets pretend everything is fine and they lead the people into thinking God is pleased with them. Jeremiah is the only prophet left who tells the truth—and the people he is preaching to don't want to listen. Still Jeremiah is faithful in giving the message (v. 16). He is the perfect example to the people. He obeys God even when everyone else doesn't. He doesn't pretend everything is OK. This kind of honesty is not popular but it is what God wants.

Is your Christian walk real before God or are you pretending? Are you faithful to God even when other Christians are not?

MONDAY • Jeremiah 7:1-11

DIGGING DEEPER Many people were traveling to the temple. Their worship wasn't going to be genuine because they were still doing all these things God told them were wrong (vv. 5-6). Jeremiah stood at the front door as people walked in and encouraged them to change. In verse 4 when the people were repeating "The temple of the Lord," it was their way of saying to Jeremiah, "We're OK." They were wrong! Just because you do things that look right or go to the right place doesn't mean you're really walking with God. Looking good on the outside doesn't cut it with God.
Is your life the same in church as it is when you're not? Are you fooling yourself into thinking you're obeying God when you aren't?

TUESDAY • Jeremiah 7:18-28

DIGGING DEEPER Today one of Judah's fake gods—"the queen of heaven" (v. 18)—is introduced. The people most likely copied this idea from the other sinful nations around them and mixed it with some rituals of making cakes and wine. Instead of just following God and what He said was true about Himself, they wanted a god they could worship by doing things. Their working to make food and other sacrifices made them part of the process rather than just servants to the God Who could do everything. Whether we realize it or not we sometimes do the same. Instead of obeying God we try to do things to please Him. We find enjoyment in other places such as people, sports, work, TV, money, or popularity.
Just because we're not worshipping hand-carved idols doesn't mean our priorities are right. What things are false gods in your life today?

WEDNESDAY • Jeremiah 8:20 - 9:9

DIGGING DEEPER Jeremiah is known as the "weeping prophet" because his heart aches for people who could be enjoying a wonderful life with their God. He refers to their sin as a sickness but there is no earthly doctor with a cure. It seems hopeless. Jeremiah feels like he would like to just run to the desert and get away from these people but he doesn't (9:2). Judah is like many people today. They go from evil to evil trying to fill a void that can only be filled by God. We ought to have the same attitude as Jeremiah did for people who don't know Christ. It should be painful to see people who don't know God but could be enjoying an awesome friendship with Him.
Who do you know that is trying to have a life without God? Do you pray for them? Ask God today to prepare opportunities for you to talk to them.

THURSDAY • Jeremiah 9:12-24

DIGGING DEEPER Verse 12 starts by asking "Who has the ability to understand?" God answers that question in verses 23-24. But in between He gives more description of coming judgment. His point is this: We may think we are wise and that we can maneuver life on earth but He is control. He is the only wise one and none of our earthly talents or riches stack up. By telling us about His wisdom God is calling us back to look at Him for understanding and guidance. Nothing else will work!
Can you think of areas in your life where you need God's understanding? Can you think of modern examples of people's earthly wisdom or wealth failing them?

FRIDAY • Jeremiah 10:1-13

DIGGING DEEPER Jeremiah shows the people how dumb it is to follow the world's ideas. In verse 2 "learning the way of the heathen" means becoming familiar with false religions. They are vain, futile, and worthless. There's no reason to know what these religions have; instead we should focus on the God we know is true. Jeremiah points to the lunacy of people covering wood with bits of metal and calling it "god." Then in verse 10 he explains why God alone is true and great. Throughout history pagan gods were often limited to one powerful attribute such as knowledge, fire, or weather. But our God is beyond that—He masters them all!

It's time for some deep thinking. Consider why God has to be able to do everything in verses 10-13 to truly be God. If He couldn't do a couple of these things how would it affect your faith?

SATURDAY • Jeremiah 10:14-23

DIGGING DEEPER Judah gets a clear picture of how God plans to punish the people for worshiping false gods. Verses 19-20 are what someone from Judah might say when the punishment happens. The speaker is referring to his family and not having them around anymore. Verses 21-22 are God speaking again. He gives a clue that an army from the north would come and destroy the people of Judah and leave all the cities empty. Verse 23 says we can't know how to walk and avoid such destruction without God. We need God to show us how to live and we need to follow the directions He gives us in His Word.

Do you ever feel like you can figure out by yourself what you should be doing in life? How often do you ask God for His help? What does verse 23 say about this?

WEEK 21

Sometimes life is hard but rarely is it as hard as Jeremiah had it. Just to prove a point, God has him do some pretty strange things this week. If Jeremiah could handle these ups and downs surely we can! It's your turn at bat—what will you do?

PRAYER FOCUS FOR THIS WEEK

THE QUESTION: What is the writer saying?
THE ANSWER: How can I apply this to my life?

SUNDAY • Jeremiah 12:1-17

DIGGING DEEPER In verse 4 the question is "Why do the wicked prosper?" Jeremiah was trying to live right and it sure didn't seem fair! Verses 7-13 are God's answer: It's only for a short time. The wicked never last! Although these wicked people were going to be punished God would not destroy all of them completely because He's still compassionate. Proverbs 13:15 says "The way of the transgressor is hard." Even when things seem to be going well for the wicked God says their prosperity won't be forever.

Do you envy unsaved people? What do you have of value that they don't? How can you help them have eternal prosperity?

MONDAY • Jeremiah 13:1-11

DIGGING DEEPER This is an action sermon. God used the waistband or linen belt as an example. It was supposed to be worn really close to the midsection. That's how God wanted to be to Judah. But Israel didn't stay close to God and what was once clean, good-looking, and brand-new became old, worn-out, and useless. That's what happens when we don't stay close to God. We become just another Christian who isn't useful to the Master. (See 2 Timothy 2:20-21.) There are already too many marred and dirty believers. What God is looking for are those who will walk close to Him and obey Him completely.

How close are you to God? When you get farther away from Him can you see how it affects your life? What can you do to stay close to Him today?

TUESDAY • Jeremiah 14:7-22

DIGGING DEEPER Have you ever been really sorry for something you did but were still punished anyway? In verses 7-9 Jeremiah confesses sin but verse 10 says God wouldn't accept it! While God wants us to be sorry for our sin He really wants us to obey in the first place. When we don't obey, punishment for sin awaits. Deuteronomy 28:15 was Judah's warning. The people knew exactly what would happen if they forgot God. Confessing sin is always right but that doesn't mean we always escape the punishment. Sometimes the only way we learn is by being punished.

Have you ever been tempted to make the same mistake twice? What punishment happened last time? Isn't it easier to just do what is right?

WEDNESDAY • Jeremiah 15:1-2, 11-16

DIGGING DEEPER Moses and Samuel are mentioned in today's passage—two men who often begged God to save His people in the past. God still had to bring punishment though (v. 2). Check out God's promise to Jeremiah in verse 11. Hard times were coming but God still promised protection for the remnant—those who believed in Him and obeyed. Even though no one else is following God we always can. He will take care of us. The question is "Who do I want to please—God or myself?" We can either enjoy the promise of verse 11 or the difficulty of verse 2. It should be a no-brainer but too often we harden our hearts and choose the wrong way.

How determined are you to follow God when others don't? Would you rather go with the crowd of verse 2 or enjoy the promise of verse 11?

THURSDAY • Jeremiah 17:1-13

DIGGING DEEPER What would you rather be: a scrawny dying bush with no water or a tree planted by streams? The answer is obvious but it's not always that easy. Many Christians miss God's blessing every day. They choose to miss out. Why? Verse 9! It is very easy to trick ourselves into thinking we're following God when we're really following our own wants. Our hearts just like to go after bad stuff. We need to have God search our hearts and show us who we're really following. Verse 10 is a great prayer for every day. We don't want to be like verse 5 and trust ourselves. We need to ask God to show us where our desires really are—for Him or for ourselves.

Knowing God and obeying Him starts with making sure our hearts are set on Him. Would you pray that God will show you your true desires?

FRIDAY • Jeremiah 18:1-12

DIGGING DEEPER Have you ever worked with clay? What's easier to work with, the hard stuff or the soft stuff? In God's hands Israel was the hard stuff (v. 12). The people had stubborn hearts that couldn't be molded in God's hands. Yes, God can do anything but He also gives us the choice to accept Him. He wants us to willingly be soft-hearted. Who would you rather trust with the sculpture of your life—the Master (God) or the amateur?

What part of your life is not submitted to God? What are the things you're really stubborn about? What should you give to God today?

SATURDAY • Jeremiah 20:7-18

DIGGING DEEPER Have you ever had a day where one minute things were great and the next things were lousy? Up and down, up and down. Jeremiah had tough days too. Verses 7-8 are the tough part. He feels like quitting. But in verse 9 he's very passionate about sharing God's Word—he's up. Verse 10 he's down. Verse 11 he's up. Verses 14-18 he's down. Are you getting seasick? The important thing is that every time he's down he turns back to God. Verse 13 is important to remember. We can always praise God and the Lord will always deliver us out of difficult situations—no matter what!

Up-and-downs are part of the Christian life. What matters is how we respond to them. Have you had some tough times this week? What did you do? What are you going to do when tough times come in the future?

WEEK 22

You probably already know that being an obedient Christian is not always the popular choice. If you think you've had it tough look at Jeremiah this week. If being an obedient Christian has been easy for you, you may need to get involved in more of God's battles. Jeremiah had guts! If he can do it, so can you!

PRAYER FOCUS FOR THIS WEEK

THE QUESTION: What is the writer saying?
THE ANSWER: How can I apply this to my life?

SUNDAY • Jeremiah 21:1-14

DIGGING DEEPER Babylon, the country that would eventually conquer Jerusalem, is getting ready to attack. The king asks Jeremiah to talk to God and find out what's going to happen. The king assumes God will protect them and he expects Jeremiah to tell him that. Jeremiah doesn't have good news for anyone but he didn't cover it up. He told the king exactly what God wanted him to. It wasn't popular but Jeremiah was faithful to God.

Who do you want to please first, God or your friends? What practical things can you do in your life today to be faithful in God's eyes that won't necessarily please the crowd?

MONDAY • Jeremiah 22:24 - 23:6

DIGGING DEEPER Coniah was the king at the time this is written but only for three months. He was taken to Babylon just like God said. His main fault was found in 23:1-2. The leaders of Judah did not help their people. Coniah and the kings before him had no desire to obey God and they led the whole country to disobey Him. Even with all this disobedience, God was still making a plan of forgiveness and reconciliation for His people. In verses 5-6 He starts talking about Jesus Himself— over 500 years before He would even be born! Coniah's *wrong* was big and so was his punishment. But Jesus' *right* was even bigger and so is His reward!
What can you do to lead your friends in a right direction today? Do you follow everybody else like Coniah or do you honor God?

TUESDAY • Jeremiah 23:25-40

DIGGING DEEPER Jeremiah wasn't the only prophet around but he was the only one telling the truth. In verse 28 God uses chaff and wheat as a metaphor. Wheat was used to make bread but it had to be crushed first. The crushed wheat was put to use but the dust and other stuff left over was called "chaff." It had no purpose. God says that's what lies are compared to the truth. God's Word and truth are powerful (fire and hammer) but anything that goes against them is just a useless lie. It will be separated out and destroyed. Many people are like this today, not following God's Word. They cloud up the truth with what they think is true.
Can you think of anything being taught today that you would classify as being lies—something that should be separated from the truth so it doesn't mislead people? Ask God to help you separate out His truth in your life.

DIGGING DEEPER God uses this example of two baskets of fruit to explain what will happen to those who follow Him and those who don't. Judah was going to be judged no matter what; but God still had a plan to protect those who followed Him. The people of Judah would go to Babylon but God had a plan to bring a remnant back. Even when God allows punishment in our lives He wants to bless us again. We can either get mad and make matters worse or we can repent and allow Him to bless us when it's time. Humbly confessing our sin is always the right response for us.
God still wants to bless us even if we're in a time of punishment. Is there a situation in your life right now where you're pushing against God? How can you be patient and rejoice in Him until this season is over?

THURSDAY • Jeremiah 25:1-12

DIGGING DEEPER Verse 3 says Jeremiah had been speaking to these people for 23 years and they still weren't listening. You can count how many times in this passage that it says they didn't listen. After warning them so many times God is introducing the kingdom of Babylon as His latest tool to bring His people back to Him. In verse 9 he calls Babylon His "servant" because with Judah ignoring God's other methods Babylon's oppression would now point the people back to God. In verse 12 however, God makes it clear that throughout all this Babylon won't be in control—they are just a tool and God will judge them one day too.
In what areas of your life would God say "You haven't listened?" How many tools is He going to have to use in your life to point you back to Him?

FRIDAY • Jeremiah 26:1-16

DIGGING DEEPER "Shiloh" (v. 9) refers to a city that existed 700 years before. Like the people of Judah the people of Shiloh didn't obey God. Shiloh also had a temple of God within the city and its people thought that they would be protected from any judgment because of that temple. They were wrong! When Jeremiah says the same thing will happen to Jerusalem it's serious business! Still, the priests responded just like the ones in Shiloh. They got angry at Jeremiah and arrested him rather than listening, examining themselves, and repenting.

Have you ever been warned or confronted and "gone on the offensive" against the person instead of dealing with your sin? God holds us responsible for our wrong especially if we've been warned. Ask Him to search your life and show you any problem areas you have right now.

SATURDAY • Jeremiah 27:1-15

DIGGING DEEPER Remember God's way of protecting the people that wanted to obey Him? He wanted them to go to Babylon. Apparently Jerusalem and the nations around them (v. 3) were planning to join forces and rebel against Babylon. Bad move! A yoke (v. 11) was a large piece of wood that went over necks of two oxen. It would hold the two side by side and force them to work together in order to pull a plow. Any ox in a yoke was forced to do work. It was in bondage. Jerusalem would be bound to the will of these people if it joined forces with them. Jeremiah was telling the nations that the only way to survive was to go to Babylon and be subject to them. That was God's will for them even though it seemed odd.

Is God asking you to do something that seems strange? Are you willing to stand alone like Jeremiah even though it's not popular?

WEEK 23

So far Jeremiah has been sharing a lot of bad news. But God still wants to bless His children even in hard times. You'll see a change in what God is telling His people this week. Even when things are difficult God is working it out for our good! Hang in there!

PRAYER FOCUS FOR THIS WEEK

THE QUESTION: What is the writer saying?

THE ANSWER: How can I apply this to my life?

SUNDAY • Jeremiah 28:1-17

DIGGING DEEPER Verse 6 is Jeremiah's way of telling the people he'd like to give them good news but he can only tell them what God says. Hananiah gave great news but unfortunately, it was all a lie. It was easy for Hananiah to say those things because it was what everyone wanted to hear. Hananiah compromised God's Word and in verse 17 we can see what happened. He was accepted and loved for a short time but his earthly popularity was no good when God decided to show Who was in charge.

Do you search for the truth even if it's not what you want to hear? How do you deal with teaching or correction that you may not feel like hearing?

MONDAY • Jeremiah 29:1-14

DIGGING DEEPER At one point over 3,000 people were taken from Jerusalem to live in Babylon. That's a long way from home! Some prophets among these people told them they'd be back in Jerusalem in no time. Once again, false prophets told the people what they wanted to hear. But Jeremiah reminded the people what to do as part of God's plan for protecting them (vv. 5-7). Verse 11 is the key for today. God always has a good plan for us. Sometimes that's hard to believe but God's design is always perfect. Even when things don't seem right or fair God can work it out for good (Romans 8:28).

What seems bad in your life right now? Do you believe God is really going to use it for good? Will you commit to looking for the good now?

TUESDAY • Jeremiah 30:1-11

DIGGING DEEPER These verses are where God told Jeremiah to write this book—the very words you're reading right now. In verse 3 God says again that the people would be brought back from their 70-year captivity and this would happen for both Israel *and* Judah. But only Judah came back. The rest of these verses look ahead to a time in the future called "The Tribulation." Everything Jeremiah had told the people so far had come true, so we can trust that what God says here will too. In these verses God still has a very specific plan for His people (vv. 7-11). Notice how God isn't just promising an escape hatch—these verses describe the relationship He was still pursuing with His people.

Even as His people are punished and go away from Him God keeps after them! Do you want a relationship with God like verses 10-11 promise?

WEDNESDAY • Jeremiah 31:1-14

DIGGING DEEPER Have you ever had a time when you were stranded far from home for a while? Maybe you had to wait somewhere strange just wanting a change of clothes and some good food. That's how Israel was feeling in these verses. God continues His promise to bring the people back to their land. He is going to build up the nation and make it beautiful and there will be much joy. In verse 9 the people are described as willingly coming back to God then. As they return He will guide them. Look at the many things God promises in these verses—how good would that be to someone stumbling home, tired and hungry?

Sometimes we don't feel like we're far from God until our sin has really gotten out of hand. But what God has in store for us is so much greater than wherever we've exiled ourselves. Do you need to return to God today?

THURSDAY • Jeremiah 31:31-40

DIGGING DEEPER The Jews lived under the old covenant, the Ten Commandments which were guidelines God had them keep so they'd focus on Him. But God never wanted His relationship with men to be a bunch of rules. The point of the Ten Commandments or the Law was to show the people their need for God so they'd put their faith in Him. They followed these rules and trusted God as He prepared the way for the fulfillment of their faith—the Savior, Jesus Christ. With this new covenant (vv. 33-34) God is looking forward to the day when people won't need rules but instead will just know Him and follow Him. We won't need to share the Gospel (v. 34) because we'll all know God personally!

Heaven and a time where everyone knows God are a long way off but the Bible says we can still know God now. Who will you tell about Him today?

FRIDAY • Jeremiah 32:1-15

DIGGING DEEPER Today God was showing Israel a special blessing. Judah was all locked up in the city of Jerusalem. The king of Babylon was right outside the city walls ready to take the king captive! Jeremiah is basically a prisoner and things don't look promising. In verse 7 Jeremiah is told to buy a field. The only reason he would do that would be to work it and grow crops—which doesn't make sense if they're all about to be captured. God was telling them even though they'd soon be taken captive "Someday you will come back to your land, and you will enjoy a peaceful life of farming. Things will change and be good for you again."

Do you see God as being good to you *all* the time? Would you pray and tell God you trust His plan for you, even when it doesn't make sense?

SATURDAY • Jeremiah 32:16-27

DIGGING DEEPER This is a prayer of Jeremiah. He starts by worshiping God; then acknowledges that God sees everything man does and knows how he thinks (v. 19). He remembers Israel's history. God brought the people of Israel out of Egypt and gave them this great land. But they still failed to obey and worship Him. That's why the city was about to be taken. In verse 25 Jeremiah questions God's instruction to buy a field. God's answer in verse 27 is "I can do anything!" God is telling Jeremiah to trust Him. Even though Jeremiah had a better track record of trusting God than the people of Israel did, he still struggled with being at peace with God's ways.

Is there anything confusing in your life right now? Would you commit to believing God can do anything in your life even when it's confusing?

WEEK 24

The key to this week is example—that's what you'll see in Jeremiah's life. He was a good example even when it was rough. You'll also get introduced to a Bible hero you've probably never heard of. If you want to see how to follow God when things are tough this week is definitely for you!

PRAYER FOCUS FOR THIS WEEK

THE QUESTION: What is the writer saying?

THE ANSWER: How can I apply this to my life?

SUNDAY • Jeremiah 32:28-44

DIGGING DEEPER In this study have you thought God was being unfair or too harsh to His people? Verses 28-35 make it understandable. God waited a long time before He brought the punishment, considering all that they did. They even sacrificed their own children to foreign gods! God was very patient. And amazingly despite all this sin God was still going to bring them back. God punished those that needed to be punished and rescued those that needed to be rescued. It's often easy for us to just look at the bad we're dealing with and ignore all the horrible things we've done against God. Still in the end He promises restoration.

It's often easy for us to just look at the bad we're dealing with and ignore all the horrible things we've done to God. Can you list some areas where he's shown mercy to you recently?

MONDAY • Jeremiah 33:1-13

DIGGING DEEPER What if you had to walk around with a rotten onion under your nose for the rest of your life? After a while life would start to stink, right? Things were getting kind of tough for Jeremiah. Almost all of his messages said something about destruction and death. Life was starting to stink! In these verses God basically tells him to see beyond the onion. Verse 3 is the key. We often need to ask God to show us the great things He is going to do. Life may be hard now but there's much more to come! It's easy to be negative and look at the bad stuff all the time. God tells us here about all the great things that are coming. Look beyond your onion today! **At the moment what stinks in your life? What good might come from it? Would you ask God to help you see the good things He has planned?**

TUESDAY • Jeremiah 33:14-26

DIGGING DEEPER Since you've been alive how often have day and night come? They're pretty consistent aren't they? Every day there is night then day and night then day. God's point here is that He set up day and night and if we can be sure about them we can be certain about the rest of His promises. Jeremiah and his people were starting to doubt. Things looked pretty bad. As the people start to wonder God uses that example of night and day then points forward to the ultimate hope. Verse 15 says Jesus is coming to even everything out! **What are some things you question God about? What promises did He make with you through His Word that are true? Do you need His help today to remind you that He's in control and His promises will come true?**

WEDNESDAY • Jeremiah 35:1-6, 12-19

DIGGING DEEPER In these verses God uses people from a particular family to show Israel what it means to obey Him. This family had been told to stay away from wine and they had. That was faithfulness! Unfortunately the people of Judah were doing just the opposite. They were the perfect example of being unfaithful to God. God rewards this family for its obedience but His punishment for Judah is harsh.

Could your life be used as an example for other believers of faithfulness or obedience? Is there a part of your life where you are disobeying God or where you've not been faithful? What should you do about it?

THURSDAY • Jeremiah 38:1-13

DIGGING DEEPER This is where things really get tough for Jeremiah. The king's officials had it in for him. Jeremiah was telling them how to be rescued: "Go to Babylon." Everyone else in the city would die. But they threw him in a well with no water. Another one of the king's officials steps in. Here's a new Bible hero for you: Ebed-melech. He didn't care what the others did. He knew that this was no way to treat one of God's prophets. We may not be the ones chosen to lead God's people or speak a controversial message but we can certainly support those who do. Godly leaders need Ebed-melechs to help them today. We need to stick up for what's right!

Are you afraid of standing for truth because of persecution from friends? Are you willing to help fellow Christians who are being persecuted?

FRIDAY • Jeremiah 39:1-2, 11-18

DIGGING DEEPER This is it! In today's verses the city was taken. It happened just like Jeremiah had told the king and all the people. In the many chapters to come you see the terrible things that happen to Judah. But notice that when the city is broken into, two people are not harmed: Jeremiah and Ebed-melech. Jeremiah had preached for 41 years to all types of people. Few had responded but one did. God protected Ebed-melech for following Him and doing what was right. You will never regret following God even when the stakes are high! Here are two guys that proved it!

Will you commit to standing for Christ even when it's not popular? Will you choose to not be afraid of how people respond to your choices to follow God?

SATURDAY • Jeremiah 50:1-7, 17-20

DIGGING DEEPER God fulfills His promises to Judah. Jeremiah prophesied that Babylon would be destroyed to show again that He punishes sin. But amidst all this talk of judgment, God's point is not destruction. Look at verse 19—the goal of all this is to bring God's people back to where they should be, in a right relationship with Him. Pain, judgment, punishment—blessings, blessings, good times, enjoyment—all things are tools God uses to draw us to Him.

What is your response as God looks to pull you back to Him? Do you fight Him? Do you chafe under His guidance? Do you complain when He corrects you? When God talks about Him satisfying us (v. 19) is that something you yearn for?

WEEK 25

Here in the first few chapters of Acts the apostles witnessed Christ's resurrection and then His ascension to Heaven. Ten days later, the Holy Spirit empowered them to take the Gospel to the whole world, and the church was born! This book is packed full of exciting true stories about what God did in and through people.

PRAYER FOCUS FOR THIS WEEK

THE QUESTION: What is the writer saying?
THE ANSWER: How can I apply this to my life?

SUNDAY • Acts 1:1-11

DIGGING DEEPER For 40 days after His resurrection Jesus instructed and encouraged His disciples about the power of the Holy Spirit. Believers would need this power for witnessing. Jesus also told them where they should go with their message of hope. Notice verses 6-8. The disciples wanted to know "the plan"— when certain prophecies would be fulfilled. Jesus told them that God would take care of that (v. 7). Their focus was to be on sharing about Him (v. 8).

For all the parts of life we haven't figured out, God has been pretty clear about how He wants us to share Him with others. Is witnessing an active part of your Christian life? What does verse 8 say about where you get power when you're telling people about God?

MONDAY • Acts 1:12-26

DIGGING DEEPER After Jesus ascended to Heaven, the disciples walked back to Jerusalem and met with the other believers. While waiting for the power of the Holy Spirit to come, Peter takes care of some church business. A replacement needed to be found for Judas and after asking for God's help (v. 24), Matthias was chosen. Even with Jesus gone and the Holy Spirit yet to come, the disciples still had a relationship with God. They knew Who to look to for direction.

God's preferred method of empowering (the Holy Spirit) was yet to come, but God was still working in the world. He still does this today—He acts in people's lives even if they don't know Him. Have you seen God's hand in an unsaved friend's life? How can you use this to point him or her to God?

TUESDAY • Acts 2:1-13

DIGGING DEEPER Just as Jesus promised, the Holy Spirit came and filled the believers. On that day the church was established. You'll notice that a lot of strange things happen in the early church that we don't see today. For instance, the Holy Spirit fills us at salvation, but not with big bursts of wind or fire (vv. 2-3). Another unique part of the early church was the believers' ability to speak in different languages or "tongues" (see Hebrews 2:3-4). People in Jerusalem could all hear the Gospel in their own languages despite only a few Hebrew-speaking people witnessing.

Christians today don't see a lot of the miracles the early church did, but we still get to see the miracle of people receiving new spiritual life. Notice the reaction of unsaved people in verse 13. How do people attack the Gospel today? How do you react when this happens? Will you keep sharing?

WEDNESDAY • Acts 2:14-21

DIGGING DEEPER Did you ever wonder why God put you in certain situations, why you were born where you were, or why you have your looks, intelligence, interests, race, or friends? Peter, now filled with the Holy Spirit, knew exactly what to do in this situation. He was going to tell all these people about Jesus! God was at work and He was going to use Peter—the mumbling, bumbling, stumbling Peter—to preach the one sermon that would start the church.

For all Peter had been through, he knew the main point—people needed to come to Christ. Who do you know that needs to know Christ today? Is your life situation discouraging you from sharing with others? Should you ask God for encouragement today so you can share His truth?

THURSDAY • Acts 2:22-36

DIGGING DEEPER Have you ever tried to win an argument with a friend? You can't just jump in and yell your opinion. You have to start with what he already thinks is right then slowly move to what you know is true. Peter does the same thing—he takes the Jews from what they know (vv. 22-24) to what they don't. They knew Jesus as a man. Peter is saying that His miracles prove He is also God. In verses 25-31, Peter then says Jesus Christ was the Savior Who was promised in Jewish prophecy. The resurrection (vv. 32-36) is the final piece of proof that He was not only God but also the fulfillment of all these prophecies and promises.

A lot of people have background knowledge about Who Jesus was, but they don't see how all the pieces fit together. It's our job to show the connection between Him and new life. Who can you witness to today?

FRIDAY • Acts 2:37-47

DIGGING DEEPER When these people heard the truth, they knew their lives needed to change. Peter told them exactly what to do: (1) repent—to admit that the way they were living was against God and to turn to Him, and (2) be baptized—start becoming involved in church practices. Peter assures them that salvation is not limited to a certain type of person (vv. 39-40)—all are called to come to Christ. Look at verses 41-47. These people had just been saved, but they were already functioning as the body of Christ should.

Verse 37 shows us that people are ready to come to Christ but they have to hear the truth first to know where to turn (Romans 10:11-15). Can you think of any creative ways to put truth in front of people today? How can you start planting seeds to show people the path to Christ?

SATURDAY • Acts 3:1-11

DIGGING DEEPER God was at work using miracles to get the Gospel out to the entire world. Notice how Peter and John were going about their regular weekly routine when God gave them a person with a prepared heart. All Peter and John had to do was let God work through them. If Peter could witness and see lives changed, so can we. Today we have the same powerful life-changing Gospel of Jesus Christ. We can tell people about Jesus in the power of the Holy Spirit and watch spiritual cripples walk!

Whom is God going to put in your path today as you go about your daily routine? Ask God to make you sensitive to His Spirit as He puts prepared hearts in front of you.

WEEK 26

Do you want to be bold and courageous? Peter and the other apostles did things that they never imagined they could do, all through the power of the Holy Spirit. Watch the miraculous story continue to unfold in this week's quiet time.

PRAYER FOCUS FOR THIS WEEK

THE QUESTION: What is the writer saying?

THE ANSWER: How can I apply this to my life?

SUNDAY • Acts 3:12-26

DIGGING DEEPER Peter is using his opportunities to witness and serve God. Now he preaches his second sermon to the Jews who are questioning his healing of the lame man. Look at his powerful Holy Spirit-inspired words as he lays out the case against these men. They killed the Christ yet God raised Him up. God was still offering these people salvation and even the kingdom, through repentance despite their rejection of Him.

Peter looks back at Jewish history again for his message. Just as God brought blessing to the world through Abraham and the nation of Israel, the Jews were getting the first chance at the new blessing—the offer of salvation.

MONDAY • Acts 4:1-12

DIGGING DEEPER Peter's second sermon had produced many converts but now his message brings persecution. Any time God is at work we know that our enemy, Satan, will be at work as well. He does his best to stop God's work and destroy God's people. Peter had previously denied Jesus in the house of Annas and Caiaphas (John 18). Now filled with the Holy Spirit, he boldly proclaims Jesus as Messiah and the only name "whereby we must be saved." Living for Jesus is a supernatural business. God alone, through His Spirit can give us the power to stand for Him.
Why not ask God to empower you so that you will have boldness as Peter did?

TUESDAY • Acts 4:13-22

DIGGING DEEPER People who have been with Jesus can't stop talking about Him! It was obvious that the miracle of healing was real because the man who had been healed was right there in the middle of the crowd of those who believed. The religious leaders also picked up on the fact that Peter and John had been with Jesus and were the real deal. They had no way to argue that the disciples' testimonies or miracles weren't true so they threatened them. They told them not to speak about Jesus. Peter and John's answer was that they couldn't stop—what they had seen and heard was just too good.
What about you? Have you been in trouble for speaking too much about Jesus? Why not try it this week? Just talk about Jesus everywhere you go. Use His name and watch the reaction of everyone around you.

DIGGING DEEPER There is a constant need to be filled with the Holy Spirit. The church couldn't do all it was called to do on its own; it had to be God working. As the believers heard the threats against them they called on the God they knew, listing what He'd done throughout history for those who followed Him. In verse 29 they ask for boldness. They knew God could work through them—now they just had to get going! Notice at the end of this passage that God's power wasn't just for them sharing the Gospel. He also gave it to them for everyday life. Even something as basic as being unselfish with our possessions is under the power of God.

We know God can do amazing things but we often need help letting Him work through us. Do you need boldness for witnessing? How about help with having an unselfish spirit? How can you ask God for this today?

THURSDAY • Acts 5:1-11

DIGGING DEEPER Ananias and Sapphira are a stark example of how the church is holy and should not be treated lightly. As drastic as this story seems you can probably think of instances in your church when someone tried to do something to look like he was serving God when it was really just a big show. God isn't zapping people on the spot today but He has promised that all sin will be punished. It is between us and God as to whether we are being honest (v. 3). For Christians, "It is a fearful thing to fall into the hands of the living God" (Hebrews 10:31).

Is there an area in your life where you are trying to look like you're doing the right thing when you're really not? Do you need to confess to others or God that your heart hasn't been right?

FRIDAY • Acts 5:12-23

DIGGING DEEPER God's work through the apostles was causing so much trouble for the Jewish leaders that they decided to throw the apostles into prison. But the balance of power has permanently been moved! God is in control and He wasn't finished with these apostles. After the angel released the apostles in the middle of the night he instructed them to go and speak "all the words of this life" in the temple. God has a message that He wants carried to the entire world and He uses us to take it.

No earthly power can interrupt what God wants to use us for. In what areas is God leading you to serve? To whom has He been guiding you to witness? What's stopping you?

SATURDAY • Acts 5:24-32

DIGGING DEEPER The religious leaders were taken aback by the audacity of the disciples. These guys just wouldn't obey them (v. 28)! Peter's answer was simple: The believers were following God not men. Notice that the apostles had a very clear idea of what God was asking them to do. Christians have had problems throughout history where they charged into situations in God's name with the result often being disaster. But the apostles were so clear on their calling that they had no problem saying "no" here in good conscience to the authorities of their day.

We can have boldness in pushing forward with our message and maybe even standing up to our authorities if we have a clear understanding of what God has called us to do. What can you do today to better know what God is asking you to do both individually and as part of the church?

This week in your quiet time you will find story after story of weak men who became bold because of the power of God. Read these pages and pray that God will use and empower you as He did those ordinary men.

PRAYER FOCUS FOR THIS WEEK

THE QUESTION: What is the writer saying?

THE ANSWER: How can I apply this to my life?

SUNDAY • Acts 5:33-42

DIGGING DEEPER The world wants to silence the Christian and even put him to death. God used Gamaliel, a religious Jew, to save the apostles' lives. They were threatened, beaten, and forbidden to speak in the name of Jesus, but when they were let go they rejoiced and started talking immediately about Christ—publicly (in the temple) and privately (in every house). They were simply being what God asked them to be: witnesses. When God says *go*, man cannot say *stop*.

What does it take to stop you from talking about Jesus? Are you talking about Jesus publicly, privately, and at every opportunity?

MONDAY • Acts 6:1-15

DIGGING DEEPER This chapter tells about the first seven deacons chosen to serve in the church. These were all very capable men but they were willing to do basic tasks because they knew that was what was needed. They had a reputation of honesty and were full of the Holy Spirit and wisdom (v. 3). By serving, deacons allowed the apostles to pray, study, and preach the Word without distraction. Stephen, one of the first deacons, was even singled out for persecution.

Whether it is a deacon in the church or in another service position, God is looking for people willing to help. He wants us to put aside our "rights" or positions we think we're entitled to because of our talents and find a place to serve others. Can you think of a place that needs your help today? Do you ever consider yourself "overqualified" to help in the church?

TUESDAY • Acts 7:1-16

DIGGING DEEPER In these verses Stephen preaches the longest sermon in the book of Acts. He proves his faith and his knowledge of the Scriptures as he traces Israel's history, starting with Abraham. His message tells about the disobedience of the Jewish people throughout history. But God was always good and His guidance is also told in story after story. Just as God was merciful and longsuffering toward Israel, He is toward us today as well.

How is God leading in your life today? Do you see Him at work in the circumstances of your life? Are you following Him in obedience?

WEDNESDAY • Acts 7:17-29

DIGGING DEEPER Stephen's sermon continues. He talks about the life of Moses. God was working in the circumstances of Moses' life to develop him into a man who would be used to deliver the people from slavery in Egypt. Moses was sinful and fearful yet God chose to use him for a purpose much bigger than himself. These testimonies of people God has used throughout history show us that He can use us, too. He is not limited by our weaknesses.

Do you struggle with your weaknesses? Do you wonder if God could ever use you? Take time to read the story of Moses today and ask God to encourage you through it.

THURSDAY • Acts 7:30-43

DIGGING DEEPER God's personal redemption in people's lives is a mirror image of His plan to redeem Israel. The reason so many early believers used the story of the nation of Israel as they share the Gospel is because the Jews would have been familiar with it. The Jewish people knew how Israel disobeyed, worshiped other gods, and had to be rescued by God. Stephen is trying to show them that the constant turning away of the Old Testament Jews was the same as their personal rejection of Jesus Christ that day.

It's easy for us to shake our heads at Israel. They worshiped idols and they never got the message! But don't we do the same thing? Can you think of areas in your life where you've acted like Israel?

FRIDAY • Acts 7:44-60

DIGGING DEEPER Stephen gets to the climax of his message in verse 48. The God that Israel served, the same God that these angry religious leaders said they served, was not like other gods. He didn't live in a temple and He wasn't pleased by sacrifices of good works. This God lived in people's *hearts*. He wanted a relationship with people through their faith in Him. But as Israel had in the past, these people were rejecting His offer (v. 51). Verse 54 says the response of these men was they were "cut to the heart"—they knew *exactly* what he was saying. They didn't like being convicted; they wanted to keep living as they were.

Stephen could have been diplomatic and fudged his message so it didn't seem so offensive. Instead he confronted these men and made them decide. Is there anyone you know who needs God's truth?

SATURDAY • Acts 8:1-13

DIGGING DEEPER In Acts 1:8 Jesus said the Gospel would spread beyond Jerusalem. We see it starting to move to Samaria and "the uttermost parts of the earth" in today's passage. Persecution was the vehicle for the rapid spreading of truth. The attacks on Christians scattered them all over, meaning even more people heard their message. While this time was great for church growth and creating missionaries we also see people using the church for their own purposes (vv. 9-13). While Stephen is the ultimate example of Christ-like sacrifice, hypocrites are the worst—they use truth and twist it for selfish purposes.

Christ's truth can be used for great purposes or bad. Do you use pressure to live one way in front of some people and another way around others?

Is your world filled with people who seem impossible to reach? This week you will read about the Gospel affecting a devil worshiper, a powerful treasurer of a nation, a possible murderer, and a military officer. The Gospel can touch the hardest heart so it can touch the hearts of your friends.

PRAYER FOCUS FOR THIS WEEK

THE QUESTION: What is the writer saying?

THE ANSWER: How can I apply this to my life?

SUNDAY • Acts 8:14-25

DIGGING DEEPER Philip had been performing miracles and many people were believing and being baptized. Then Peter and John came from Jerusalem and the Holy Spirit was given to these new believers. Simon, who knew a lot about earthly powers of magic and trickery, wanted this power, too. Peter uses some pretty blunt words as he describes why Simon can't have it (vv. 20-23). He knew that the power for miracles came from God and for specific purposes. It wasn't supposed to be a circus-like attraction or a way to draw in big crowds that wouldn't be interested in the Gospel. God used these gifts and miracles in specific ways to share the Gospel and grow the church.

Do you ever find yourself wanting God's power so you can look better? What does Peter say about this?

MONDAY • Acts 8:26-40

DIGGING DEEPER Have you ever felt God asking you to leave your group of friends and reach out to someone who was alone? God led Philip out of a great revival meeting in Samaria to witness to one prepared heart in the desert. The eunuch was a man of great authority in Egypt who had been looking for God in Jerusalem and couldn't find Him. Philip used the base of knowledge the man already had from Isaiah (53:7-8) and led the man to Christ.

What do you do when the Holy Spirit leads you to witness to people outside of your comfort zone? Why not pray right now and ask God to give you a person with a prepared heart to whom you can witness today?

TUESDAY • Acts 9:1-9

DIGGING DEEPER Of all the people you know who do you think is the most unlikely to get saved? If you were living back in these days you would think it was Saul of Tarsus! Saul hated Christians and he thought he was serving God by persecuting them. He worked with the religious leaders who refused to consider that Jesus was the answer, the fulfillment of prophecy. When the light came however, Saul was suddenly face-to-face with that Jesus. Jesus called him out for what he had been doing and Saul began his first step toward personally knowing the Christ that was the answer to the Scripture he'd been studying his whole life.

Often when we've studied something we can be blind to new evidence. Are there any parts of your Christian life that you're holding on to even if God is convicting you and telling you to take a second look?

WEDNESDAY • Acts 9:10-22

DIGGING DEEPER It's one thing when we see God use someone who is very talented or when God chooses to use us. But what happens when He picks someone who has been horrible to us or other Christians? Many times we suffer from the "older brother" syndrome (Luke 15:11-32)—we are resentful when the prodigal sons get the same blessings as those who have been obeying all along. In Acts today though, we see the perfect attitude. Ananias does not judge Paul or refuse to do what God asks. He takes a minute to clarify (vv. 13-14) then goes straight into what looks like a dangerous situation.

Do you ever struggle with who God chooses to do His work? Is there an attitude of selfishness or bitterness you need to deal with? Who can you ask to help you with this?

THURSDAY • Acts 9:23-31

DIGGING DEEPER God started using Paul for His work but it wasn't without a time of training first. Galatians 1:17-24 explains that Paul spent three years in Arabia studying Scripture and praying before he became a spiritual powerhouse. God used this time to clean up his old misconceptions of the Bible and Himself and instead show him what a real relationship with Christ was. With this time of preparation Paul was ready not only to preach and write letters of doctrine to the church, he was also primed for persecution (v. 23). Notice how God provided Barnabas (v. 27) as an early ally for Paul's work.

Sometimes God wants to prepare us in specific ways before we jump into ministry. How can you use Bible study and prayer to get to know Him more personally today?

DIGGING DEEPER The spotlight now turns back on Peter. The Gospel is being shared and the apostles are moving between the churches in Jerusalem, Judea, Galilee, and Samaria. The apostles had great miracle-working power that was used to spread the Gospel. Every time they performed a miracle people were brought to Christ (vv. 35, 42). Now Peter moves into the house of Simon the tanner, a man who cured animal skins. This was a place a Jew would not normally go because of Old Testament laws about touching animals but it was God's launching pad for the church to go to the uttermost part of the earth (1:8).

The places God was starting to take the apostles were certainly outside their comfort zone. Is there somewhere God is asking you to go that you aren't feeling great about? Are you willing to pray about going to them?

SATURDAY • Acts 10:1-8

DIGGING DEEPER Today's verses tell the amazing story of the first Gentile being converted to Christ. Cornelius is a Roman officer in charge of 100 men. His heart is seeking God but he doesn't know where to find Him. But God sets up someone to send to him. He would seem like an unlikely person to become a convert but God had other plans!

People can hear about God through TV, radio, or books. They can pick up the Bible or seek out a church. But most times that's not enough. To get a fully clear picture of God and what they have to do to be saved they need someone to personally show them. Who can you seek out today that may need some direction? Are you willing to go to places where people just need someone to explain the Gospel to them?

WEEK 29

Acts is the "power book" of the Bible. Story after story shows God working in the world. From Cornelius' miraculous salvation to Peter's release from prison, we see God working to get the Gospel to the ends of the earth. Be prepared for more exciting news as lives are changed.

PRAYER FOCUS FOR THIS WEEK

THE QUESTION: What is the writer saying?

THE ANSWER: How can I apply this to my life?

SUNDAY • Acts 10:9-22

DIGGING DEEPER Peter thought that only Jews could be saved but God shows him that Gentiles can be saved too. Tradition is one of the biggest hurdles we face in the Christian life ("We've always done it this way"). The vision of the sheet full of unclean animals and the instruction from God to "kill and eat" broke down all the Jewish traditions that Peter had practiced throughout his life. God was using a very real example to help Peter understand that Christ was all that mattered now. The Law and the special work with Israel had been helpful in pointing people to God, but now that the Savior had come it was time to point all of mankind to Christ.

Can you think of any traditions in your church, home, or personal life that may be keeping you from really serving Christ? Do certain ways you do things ever keep you from reaching out to people?

MONDAY • Acts 10:23-33

DIGGING DEEPER If only we knew the work God was doing in the hearts of people we would be more willing witnesses. God led Peter to go to Cornelius and Peter had to act on what the Spirit had led him to do. God was breaking down Peter's prejudice (v. 28) and was bringing a large group of family and friends into the kingdom (vv. 24, 33). The stage was now set for the power of the Gospel to take over!

We all want to see God do big things but we often resist His direction if our role doesn't seem that big or great. Why is it important to obey God even in the small tasks? Where can you choose to obey Him today?

TUESDAY • Acts 10:34-48

DIGGING DEEPER Peter's message to Cornelius was the same message that we share when we witness. People must believe that Jesus is God (v. 36). He came to earth as a human (v. 38). He lived a perfect life, was crucified, was buried, and rose again. He was seen by many people (vv. 39-40). The requirement for salvation is shared in verse 43: "whosoever believeth." The path to Christ is the same today. We must give people knowledge of Who God is so they have a chance to believe.

Just as Peter shared with these Gentiles without being sure why God wanted him to, we need to share with all types of people so they have the chance to believe. Who can you think of today who may not have heard the Gospel? Who do you know who needs to hear more about Who Jesus is?

WEDNESDAY • Acts 11:1-15

DIGGING DEEPER Just as God's work with the Gentiles didn't make sense to Peter, it also didn't make sense to other Christians when they found out. Peter took time to think his words through and prepare his message (v. 4). He explained what God had done and used His words to make the argument. He also told how God gave the Gentiles the same sign that the Jews received on the day of Pentecost (v. 15).
We may face criticism from others, even Christians, for our choices. But if we know our direction has been from God our first step should be to point people back to Him. How can you prepare your answers for others today in case you are asked about your relationship with God?

THURSDAY • Acts 11:16-30

DIGGING DEEPER Peter finishes his testimony about the salvation of Cornelius in verses 16-18. The people he was talking with realized it was an act of God. The rest of today's verses center on the church at Antioch. This special church became the sending church for the Apostle Paul (still named Saul here). Barnabas was a key leader and continued to be a friend to Saul. We should all want to be like Barnabas, who was still backing Saul as he had always done (9:27). The visit mentioned here is spoken of in more detail in Galatians 2:1-10.
Barnabas was a great encourager who helped people who were following God. Can you think of a person who needs your encouragement today? How about a specific ministry that just needs someone encouraging its workers to cling to God (v. 23)?

FRIDAY • Acts 12:1-11

DIGGING DEEPER James was the first of the apostles to be martyred. After he died the king thought he would make himself even more popular with the Jews by also killing Peter. Peter was in prison at the time but God apparently wasn't ready for him to go to Heaven yet. Peter himself didn't even know what God was doing. In fact, he thought his miraculous jail release was a dream. He finally realized that he wasn't dreaming and that God was really at work in this situation all along.

Do you ever wonder why God allows one Christian to die and another to live? God has a specific purpose and plan for every life. How can you trust His plan, especially if you don't know it today?

SATURDAY • Acts 12:12-25

DIGGING DEEPER Now we're in John Mark's house (v. 12) where Peter arrived and broke up the prayer meeting. Answers to prayer sometimes catch even believers off guard. Herod, unable to accept that God had supernaturally allowed Peter to escape, had the soldiers killed. Herod wanted to show everyone that he was in control but God had the last word in his life. As Herod accepted the praise of people and had his ego boosted God struck him dead. God will not be mocked or share His glory. He will have His way in this world. Anyone who sets out to put himself in the place of God should beware!

Do you ever wonder how your prayers would be answered if they were prayed in faith? Can you remember some times when God answered your prayers? What do you need to pray for in faith today?

WEEK 30

In every area of our lives there is someone in charge to whom we have to answer. This week we see how Paul and Barnabas answer the call to preach the Gospel. They share the truth when they are persecuted and stoned and they get counsel from those in authority over them when they have questions.

PRAYER FOCUS FOR THIS WEEK

THE QUESTION: What is the writer saying?

THE ANSWER: How can I apply this to my life?

SUNDAY • Acts 13:1-13

DIGGING DEEPER We've all been in situations where someone was choosing teams. One captain chooses and then the other and so on until everyone is on a team. In today's passage we have a very distinct choice from God. The Holy Spirit Himself said, "Now separate to me Barnabas and Saul for the work to which I have called them." Paul and Barnabas already belonged to Christ and were hard at work serving God in Antioch. But God had more planned for them to go and preach the Gospel elsewhere. Notice that these men were not waiting around for some glamorous position; they were servants already doing all they could for God.

Even if God has a very specific area where He wants to use you in the future that doesn't mean you can't start serving now. Can you think of a ministry in your church that could use a helping hand?

MONDAY • Acts 13:14-25

DIGGING DEEPER Sometimes we can't wait to hear news about something that affects us, like the outcome of an election, or whether we've made the team, or passed a tough course. We wait impatiently for any news that will tell us what we are dying to know. Paul loved to tell people about Christ and to remind the Jews that Jesus was the Savior they had been looking for all these years. Paul's desire was to show that the coming of Jesus was not an accident in God's program but rather the fulfillment of His plan. The Jews rejected Christianity because they thought Jesus was imposing on God's plan but Paul wants them to know it was exactly the opposite—Jesus was the One they were looking for.
Do you ever forget to be grateful that you have found the answer and Savior that people have been looking for throughout history?

TUESDAY • Acts 13:26-41

DIGGING DEEPER God doesn't make mistakes. If He did He wouldn't be God. Paul makes that point very clear in today's passage. Three times (vv. 27, 29, and 33) Paul emphasizes that the things that happened to Jesus were not mistakes. They all happened according to the prophetic plan of God. This was an important point to Paul and it should be to us too. God always intended that Jesus should die. It was part of God fulfilling His promise. The importance of Christ's death, burial, and resurrection is seen in verses 38-39, where Paul reminds his readers that without Christ's sacrifice there would be no salvation from sin.
Have you ever questioned an area of your life where you thought God made a mistake? What helped you get through it?

WEDNESDAY • Acts 13:42-52

DIGGING DEEPER   When people lose their sight it makes everyday life almost impossible. Spiritual blindness not only blinds a person's heart and mind but also spreads this blindness to others. That's what was happening with the Jews in Antioch of Pisidia. They not only rejected the Gospel but also didn't want anyone else to accept it. For this reason Paul and Barnabas were called to take the Gospel to them. Blind people would accept the gift of sight if it was offered to them but the truth was being kept from them by those who didn't believe.

Unbelief in God doesn't just hurt the nonbeliever—it spreads to others too. Do you have any attitudes in your life that are not trusting God? Do you think this could be keeping others from trusting Him even in everyday ways?

THURSDAY • Acts 14:1-13

DIGGING DEEPER   Most of us have never had to run for our lives but every once in a while we say or do something that will get us in big trouble and we find ourselves looking for a quick exit in order to survive. Paul and Barnabas were spreading the Gospel in Iconium. Unbelieving Jews didn't like their message though so they tried to turn the crowd against Paul and Barnabas with lies. Paul and Barnabas left the city only to step into more chaos. The people of Lystra and Derbe thought they were gods come to earth because they had healed a crippled man. With much persuasion and common sense Paul told the people about the true God, and that he and Barnabas were just men here to serve Him.

What can we say and do that will make it clear to people who the true God is? Who will you speak to today?

FRIDAY • Acts 14:14-28

Q

A

DIGGING DEEPER Have you ever had one of those days when no one seemed to understand you? Things started out bad for Paul and Barnabas and then got worse! They walked right back into the mess when they got to Lystra because the Jews from Antioch and Iconium had come and persuaded the people that Paul was bad news. The people gathered rocks and stoned Paul leaving him for dead. But while the disciples from Lystra gathered around Paul, he got up and went into the city (v. 20) and the next day he and Barnabas left for Derbe. Only through God's protection did Paul survive the stoning and live to preach another day.
Can you think of specific times God has protected you? How about providing for you? What "little blessings" does He give you each day to encourage you to keep serving Him?

SATURDAY • Acts 15:1-12

Q

A

DIGGING DEEPER Have you ever wondered about some of the traditions you have at your church? Why do they do certain things the way they do? Paul and Barnabas found themselves in the middle of a controversy that took them to the high counsel in Jerusalem. Circumcision in the Old Testament was God's indication that His people, the Jews, were set apart for Him. The Gentiles were not circumcised but were still trusting in Christ as their Savior. So the question had to be answered: Is circumcision necessary for salvation? Peter gives a good defense against requiring Gentiles to observe Jewish rituals. Peter's point was that if the Holy Spirit accepted Gentiles apart from the Law and circumcision why should we as men try to require it?
What does Scripture say is required of us to be saved?

WEEK 31

Can you remember the last time you worked on a project? It takes time. There are many things to consider and if you give up midway what you've made ends up faulty or nothing is accomplished. This week we will see the importance of not giving up when things are tough.

PRAYER FOCUS FOR THIS WEEK

THE QUESTION: What is the writer saying?
THE ANSWER: How can I apply this to my life?

SUNDAY • Acts 15:13-29

DIGGING DEEPER From the Middle East to the local playground we all have to decide that we'll give up certain freedoms if we are going to live and work together with people who are different than us. In today's passage there was conflict because Christian Jews still practiced some of their cultural traditions. The Gentile Christians didn't understand why they needed to do those things, especially circumcision. James and the council from Jerusalem sent word that the Gentile Christians did not need to follow all the cultural habits of the Jews but there were a few things (v. 29) that would promote unity among all believers.

We do certain things because they help our walk with God or we think they're the right thing to do. The danger is when they become more important than people. Can you think of any examples in your life today?

MONDAY • Acts 15:30-41

DIGGING DEEPER Have you ever had an argument with a friend where you had to agree to disagree? Paul and Barnabas had a disagreement over taking Mark with them on this missionary journey because he had quit the last time they were together. Rather than continuing to disagree Paul chose Silas and Barnabas took Mark and the two pairs ministered to different people. Because Barnabas worked with Mark and gave him another chance to prove himself, Mark became useful to God and Paul in the ministry (2 Timothy 4:11). Although Paul's conviction kept them from working together at that time the conviction of Barnabas kept Mark in the ministry. God often leads Christians in different directions on the same issue.
Can you think of any situations where you need to agree to disagree and just focus on what God has asked you to do?

TUESDAY • Acts 16:1-13

DIGGING DEEPER There are a lot of things Christians do for their "testimony"—to give the world a certain idea of how Christ-followers should act. For example, many Christians don't drink certain beverages or watch certain movies because some people think those behaviors are wrong. The Bible may not condemn some actions outright but it does say that if something can be confusing to new Christians or unbelievers we shouldn't do it (1 Corinthians 8-10). That's what Paul is teaching here with Timothy and circumcision. He didn't *have* to be circumcised but it would keep people from having excuses to attack him.
Can you think of something that you or maybe your parents have done to be an example? Can you think of anything you should be doing?

WEDNESDAY • Acts 16:14-24

DIGGING DEEPER It would make quite a headline if we found out that a local drug lord was using his own money to feed the hungry and build houses for the poor. The problem with this picture is that profit from something illegal is always wrong no matter what good someone tries to do with it. Paul met a woman who was demon possessed and was a fortune teller. She spoke the truth about Paul saying that he was God's servant proclaiming salvation but these words were coming from the power of Satan in her. Truth can often come from ungodly sources but that doesn't mean we should allow or acknowledge these ungodly roots.
Areas such as science or music say a lot of true things but without the power of God behind them they cannot change lives. We need to make sure that the things we support are serving the best interests of Christ.

THURSDAY • Acts 16:25-40

DIGGING DEEPER Sometimes we suffer because we do what is right. Daniel suffered when he was thrown into the lion's den for praying to God. Christ suffered and died because of His message that He was God. Paul and Silas were beaten and put in prison because Paul cast a demon out of the slave girl causing her owners to lose money. Paul and Silas, rather than being upset that their rights were being violated, sang hymns and prayed (v. 25). Not only did the other prisoners see this great testimony but after God sent the earthquake Paul shared the Gospel with the jailer too. When people see how we handle tough situations they will often want to know why.
Do people see you trusting God? Are you different than others when it comes to worry and trust? Has anyone ever asked you about your faith?

FRIDAY • Acts 17:1-9

DIGGING DEEPER In today's passage we learn at least five important things: 1) Regular church attendance is expected. 2) We teach and learn something from the Word. 3) Expect to see people saved. (4) Anticipate some opposition; and 5) New growth will come. What we say and do always affects more than just ourselves. Paul and Silas went into the synagogue to teach Who Christ was and many Jews and Gentiles believed. But other Jews were jealous because people believed Paul instead of them. They even started a riot. The Christians did not give up though. They witnessed to others concerning their faith and the Church grew despite the opposition.

Have people ever accused you of stirring up trouble because you shared about Christ? What does today's passage say your response should be?

SATURDAY • Acts 17:10-21

DIGGING DEEPER When we watch our favorite sports team play, we realize that to be their best they cannot give up or quit. After Paul, Silas, and Timothy were thrown out of town they left Thessalonica and went to Berea to preach the Gospel. They were not about to give up. It wasn't long before the Jews from Thessalonica followed them and stirred up trouble in Berea too. So Paul went to Athens and began to reason with these people (v. 17) about Christ and His resurrection. The Greeks were deeply interested in knowledge of all kinds so they listened closely to what Paul had to say about Christ (vv. 20-21).

Paul knew that if he put the truth in front of the Greeks God would do the rest, even if the Greeks were just listening to hear something new. Who can you think of today who just needs to hear some truth about Christ?

WEEK 32

Truth keeps us from making mistakes. The chapters in this week's study are a reminder of the importance of knowing the truth about Christ and living our lives based on it.

PRAYER FOCUS FOR THIS WEEK

THE QUESTION: What is the writer saying?
THE ANSWER: How can I apply this to my life?

SUNDAY • Acts 17:22-34

DIGGING DEEPER The people of Athens had altars to all types of gods and in case they missed one, an altar for the "unknown god." Paul fills them in. Not only is this One they're missing a "God" in the true sense of the word "God" (He made the earth and can do everything—v. 24), but He's so God that He's beyond everything. Men can't physically grasp Him (v. 25) and even as they seek Him they keep missing (v. 27). This God is the source of time (v. 26) and life itself (v. 28). Best yet He's now giving men a chance to see Him. He calls them to repent (v. 30)—to turn to Him from their other attempts at religion and fulfillment.

Christianity fits in with people's questions about life and religion more than we sometimes realize. What has Christ done that other religions can't? Who can you talk to who is trying to figure out an "unknown God"?

MONDAY • Acts 18:1-17

DIGGING DEEPER We all like to know when we are doing something right. When we don't get feedback we wonder if we messed up or if no one cares. Paul met opposition when he was preaching, but he never got discouraged. Even if some would not hear him and believe he was determined to go to those who would. An added encouragement was God speaking to him in a vision. God told him to not be afraid and to continue to speak the truth because Christ was with him. There were many believers in Corinth waiting for him (vv. 9-10).

God used a vision to encourage Paul but nowadays He uses a more practical method—us! Who do you know who needs encouragement today?

TUESDAY • Acts 18:18-28

DIGGING DEEPER Have you ever watched a TV show where you get the first part but then have to wait for Part 2? You'd be silly to go around telling people that the first part was it when you hadn't heard the end of the story. That's what's happening in today's passage with Apollos. Having heard John the Baptist talk about the need for repentance, Apollos was teaching boldly in the synagogue (v. 25). He didn't know however that Jesus had brought the second half of the story. Salvation had come in Christ. Aquila and Priscilla took Apollos aside and carefully instructed him. Apollos was then used by God to refute the Jews showing them from Scripture that Jesus is the Christ (v. 28).

Today's lesson is a good reminder of how we are to patiently help new believers understand more about Christ. Whom can you help?

WEDNESDAY • Acts 19:1-10

DIGGING DEEPER As simple as the Gospel is we can see in these verses that Paul spent a lot of his ministry correcting misconceptions about the truth. Some people just hadn't had their doctrine updated (vv. 2-3). They needed new information but already had the foundational belief. Others needed some strong apologetics, or arguments, or proof to show that Christianity made sense (v. 8). Many others needed to hear the good news for the first time (v. 10).

Most people you'll encounter in your Christian walk will be at different stages of the Christian life. God's truth is applicable to all levels of spiritual growth though, and we need to teach others as well as learn new lessons ourselves. Who can you help learn more about the truth today? Is there someone you can seek out to help you?

THURSDAY • Acts 19:11-22

DIGGING DEEPER Have you ever walked past a dog and thought it was a "nice doggie" only to find out that the smile on its face was from scheming about how to eat your leg? In Ephesus there were certain men who thought it would make them popular if they could cast out demons in the name of Christ as Paul had done (v. 13). But the demon they encountered knew they had no authority and gave all seven men a good thrashing. The situation only brought respect and glory to God. Many people today do not believe the truth but still try to deceive people into believing they have authority from God. It's important that we know the difference.

The way we can know who is really teaching the truth is to compare what is being taught with the truth of Scripture. How much do you know?

FRIDAY • Acts 19:23-41

DIGGING DEEPER Remember the last time you were around a kid who pitched a fit because he didn't get his way? It goes back to our selfish nature. We think that if we don't get what we want we have the right to kick, scream, and get angry. That same selfish nature was what was getting the people in today's passage angry. They were upset over not making money from the worship of Diana now that so many people turning to God after Paul's ministry there.

We may not be worshipping idols but we certainly know what it's like to be inconvenienced. How do you react when you lose a comfort of life? Do you ever pitch fits with God because He's taken something away from you? How about when you're experiencing something tough?

SATURDAY • Acts 20:1-12

DIGGING DEEPER Verse 7 notes that the believers met on the first day of the week—Sunday. This was done because it was the day of Christ's resurrection. Most Christian churches meet on Sunday for that reason which would have been different from the Jewish tradition of meeting on the Sabbath. This practical change also had big spiritual implications. Under the New Covenant, Christians no longer had to observe the Mosaic Law. New Testament writers supported this move; they never told the church to meet on the Sabbath or to follow the many rules that had become associated with that day. The grace of Jesus Christ had brought a new way of living. **Can you think of any other reasons why Christians getting a new specific day to worship God would be important?**

WEEK 33

Someone hiring workers looks for people who are dedicated, dependable, and willing to follow directions. God expects the same from us and Paul is a great example. This week we will see the importance of being loyal to Christ and following His leading in our lives.

PRAYER FOCUS FOR THIS WEEK

THE QUESTION: What is the writer saying?

THE ANSWER: How can I apply this to my life?

SUNDAY • Acts 20:13-24

DIGGING DEEPER Paul had a goal of going to Jerusalem (v. 22) which Jesus confirmed in Acts 23:11. Notice that the passage says Paul "determined" (v. 16)—he set his mind on a specific task and moved forward. As Paul describes God's work in verses 18-24 we can see that it was anything but easy. Even now he was headed into another precarious situation where people would oppose him (v. 22). But Paul's ministry was never about himself. In verse 24 he basically says, "The bottom line is I want to do what God wants. Nothing else matters."
If you had to write an essay defending your work as a Christian what would you say? What would be your supporting arguments? Would you have any tips to pass on to other Christians?

MONDAY • Acts 20:25-38

DIGGING DEEPER We are all familiar with tests and quizzes. Mid-terms and finals keep us up at night since we want to be ready to prove that we understand our course material. Paul defends his ministry here as he examines his work. He told the church elders that he had no regrets; he had served as God had intended. He presented a summary of all he had done and then he exhorted the elders to "examine" themselves—to test themselves and take inventory of how they were watching over and protecting their congregations (vv. 28-29). Paul likened the false teachers of the day to wolves, emphasizing the importance of being on guard.

When is the last time you "determined" to do something for God? How about your view of life—can you say you don't care what happens as long as God is glorified? Will you pray for God's help with this today?

TUESDAY • Acts 21:1-14

DIGGING DEEPER In these verses Paul's friends are using their best means of persuasion to keep a hero of the faith from going into a hostile situation. In verse 11 Agabus tells Paul that if he goes to Jerusalem he'll be captured. Look at Paul's answer in verse 13. He says, "Yeah, of course I'll be bound—and they'll probably kill me, too! I'm ready!" The believers were obviously concerned. But they knew Paul was closely following God's guidance. They put their own worries in second place behind God's will (v. 14).

Our tendency with people we care about is to protect them. But God has specific purposes for each of us and we need to be willing to do—or let people we care about do—what He wants. Will you make a commitment today to do God's will first even if it endangers you or someone you love?

WEDNESDAY • Acts 21:15-26

DIGGING DEEPER We often find it hard to understand different cultures and traditions. In these verses Paul has gone to Jerusalem to give a good report about the many Gentiles who have trusted Christ and are being discipled (v. 19). Some people were spreading false reports that Paul was teaching Jewish believers to forsake their heritage, an accusation proved untrue in Acts 16:1-3 and 18:18. The elders proposed a way where Paul could show his loyalty to the traditions (vv. 23-24). Paul did not want to offend anyone so he followed their advice.

The Bible teaches that it's what's in a person's heart that matters not the way they look. But for some people physical appearance is important in Christianity. Can you think of any times this has happened with people you know? What does Paul show us that the Christ-like response is?

THURSDAY • Acts 21:27-40

DIGGING DEEPER Paul had been expecting trouble when he got to Jerusalem and today he gets it. The people were upset because in Paul's work he had associated with Greeks (v. 28). The Jews were trying to protect their religion and keep it separate from a man who preached salvation for all. Soon a mob formed and Paul had an unlikely savior—a Roman captain. The captain thought Paul was someone else—an Egyptian troublemaker—and God used this case of mistaken identity to get Paul out of a riot and into a situation where the angry Jews would have to listen to his words (v. 40).

With all the hubbub Paul didn't even get a chance to share the Gospel. Are there any situations you're dealing with where you need to not be frustrated with how things are going but instead thank God for His plan?

FRIDAY • Acts 22:1-16

DIGGING DEEPER Paul knows he's dealing with a hostile crowd but he does several things to make sure his message is heard. First, he speaks in their language (v. 2). Next, he lays out the proof of who he is and why he's qualified (v. 3). He wanted them to know he understood their doctrine and had learned from the best. Then he acknowledges their zeal for God (v. 3). Finally, he gives his testimony—a *personal* testimony of how God had saved him. He wasn't selling something he hadn't tried. He had been changed!

Have you ever used Paul's method here when witnessing? Show people you know where they're coming from and share your story of personal change. Try it today!

SATURDAY • Acts 22:17-30

DIGGING DEEPER Through careful reasoning Paul had shared the Gospel and showed these people that salvation was available to both the Gentiles and the Jews. But they didn't want to hear it. They rejected his words. Notice how Paul recounts God speaking to him personally in this situation (v. 18). Paul was one of the few New Testament believers to have an encounter like this with God. The others were Peter (10:10, 11:5) and John (Revelation 1:10).

Paul is rejected by these people but the point is that they heard the truth. They now had no excuse—no way to say they weren't aware of God's way of salvation. We can't let rejection keep us from sharing Christ. Who do you need to talk to today?

WEEK 34

Sometimes we feel like our lives are out of control. School is tough, we can't find a job, our parents are having problems, and we don't know what to do. This week we will be reminded how God uses all things for His purposes.

PRAYER FOCUS FOR THIS WEEK

THE QUESTION: What is the writer saying?

THE ANSWER: How can I apply this to my life?

SUNDAY • Acts 23:1-10

DIGGING DEEPER Paul is in the middle of a tense situation here as he stands among the spiritual leaders of Israel. He gets smacked (v. 2) then shoved around (v. 10). Ananias was one of Israel's most cruel and corrupt high priests. He shows his character by breaking Jewish law and hitting Paul (vv. 2-3; Deuteronomy 25:1-2). Paul calls attention to Ananias' sinfulness ("white wall" refers to someone who looks good on the outside but is covering up filth) then gets the Pharisees and Sadducees going by bringing up the controversial topic of the resurrection.

Paul started this meeting by sticking up for his character (v. 1) but soon realized he was among men who wouldn't care. Have you ever been in a situation where people would rather fight than listen to truth? What can you learn from Paul's example?

MONDAY • Acts 23:11-22

DIGGING DEEPER Today we see another example of God working through people to accomplish His purposes. These Jews hated Paul so much that they made a vow that they would not eat until they killed him. Paul's nephew was in the right place at the right time, led by God to be there. God then used the commander to take Paul out of a dangerous situation. God had a plan for Paul and there wasn't anything or anyone who could change that plan.
Can you think of any times when God used little details throughout the day or other people to protect you from a dangerous situation?

TUESDAY • Acts 23:23-35

DIGGING DEEPER Lysias, with knowledge of the planned assassination realizes he needs to get Paul out of Jerusalem and to his supervisor, Felix. The fact that Lysias sends half of his garrison shows just how serious the plot against Paul may have been. Every step in this process brought Paul in contact with more people of authority to whom he could witness. Lysias explained in the letter (vv. 26-30) that Paul had not broken any Roman laws. The Jews were the ones accusing Paul.
We often wonder why life isn't fair. We weren't treated right or things don't seem to even out in the end. But Paul didn't give any thought to whether it was fair that he was locked up for no reason. He just looked for situations where he could witness. His "unfair" situation brought God glory. Do you ever get upset by how unfair life seems? What should your response be?

WEDNESDAY • Acts 24:1-16

DIGGING DEEPER As the Jewish leaders make their case against him Paul has to deal with their lies. He calmly says that their accusations are not true and emphasizes that he believes many of the same things they do. Notice how the Jewish leaders accuse him of being a troublemaker. They use some pretty inflammatory words while Paul simply states his case. The leaders also say Paul was the ringleader of the Nazarenes, a sect they hoped the Roman authorities would look down on.
When someone says outrageous things about us the easy response is to yell back and show them how far off they are. Does Paul's method of defense tell us to act this way? How did he handle the pressure?

THURSDAY • Acts 24:17-27

DIGGING DEEPER Paul gets the perfect platform here to share the Gospel with a powerful leader. Felix was well aware of the politics among the Jews and their constant fighting, so he sort of understood what Paul was saying. Although Paul had to stay locked up he had some freedom. He got to minister to people (v. 23). Better yet, he got to spend time with Felix himself and explain what Christianity was all about. Paul shared some of the more demanding parts of the faith (righteousness, self-control, judgment) and Felix wasn't sure he liked what he heard.
Have you ever seen a Christian given a great chance to witness and then talks about how God forgives everyone? We can't be afraid of what people will think—we need to tell them how our God is both loving and righteous. How can you pray for opportunities for this today?

FRIDAY • Acts 25:1-12

DIGGING DEEPER A new ruler came in and the Jews started their case against Paul again. They were still worked up about Paul and his ministry but had nothing they could prove (v. 7). Festus gave Paul the chance to prove his innocence in Jewish court but Paul knew this would only favor the Jews. So he continued the plan God had given him earlier (23:11)—he asked to go to Rome.

Temptation isn't always toward wrong—often we are tempted to take the easy way out of a situation. We may see a route that looks better than the plan God originally called us to. Have you ever been tempted to take an easy way out? If you change your plans, do you spend time in prayer and make sure that's what God wants you to do?

SATURDAY • Acts 25:13-27

DIGGING DEEPER Festus gets a visit from King Agrippa and tries to explain the strange situation of one of his prisoners. Notice verses 18-19—Festus didn't understand the accusation the Jews were making. "Superstition" (v. 19) refers to the way outsiders often saw the Jewish religion—it seemed like a fear-motivated fairy tale. Festus had been surprised that all this unrest came from the question of whether this guy Jesus was alive. King Agrippa told him he'd help figure it out.

Many people don't understand Christianity—they think it's a fairy tale, a superstition, or just weird. But the early church didn't withdraw and decide to "not be in the world"—they kept explaining Christ to people and inviting them to believe. Should you be doing the same with the unsaved people you know who think Christianity is crazy? How can you do this today?

People don't pick up a book and start reading it in the middle. If we see a good film on TV but it's already partway through we'll often wait until we can see the whole thing. If we picked up Paul's story right now it wouldn't look good—but we know God has been faithful before and He will be again!

PRAYER FOCUS FOR THIS WEEK

THE QUESTION: What is the writer saying?

THE ANSWER: How can I apply this to my life?

SUNDAY • Acts 26:1-18

DIGGING DEEPER Paul's message is similar to ones we've seen before in Acts. He describes his authenticity as a Jew and how drastic it was for him to become a Christian. He makes sure they understand what it was like to be personally persuaded by Christ. Imagine how Agrippa would be listening to this and deciding if it made sense. The clincher is in verses 16-18. With this experience intact Paul had been told to share it with others. As he voices verse 18 he is saying to this powerful king, "Now it's your chance. Will you turn from darkness to light? Will you be forgiven?"

Paul simply laid out his case, shared his testimony, and pointed emphatically to Christ. Take another look through the verses and try to tie them into your life today. How can you use this example as you witness?

MONDAY • Acts 26:19-32

DIGGING DEEPER As Paul continues his defense he explains that he's done nothing but restate the Jewish prophecies and show how Jesus has fulfilled them. Suddenly Festus interrupts and calls him crazy. He's heard enough from this guy who's spent too much time with his books and claimed to be seeing visions! Notice Paul's response. He doesn't get sidetracked but instead turns to the man he knows has been listening—King Agrippa—and continues his challenge. He knows Agrippa has been following his message and realizing it all makes sense.
Agrippa's response—that he was almost persuaded—may seem discouraging but we know he at least heard the truth, which is all we are called to do (God changes hearts). Is there anyone you've been sharing the Gospel with who needs to hear the question "Do you believe?"

TUESDAY • Acts 27:1-13

DIGGING DEEPER Today's passage gives us a few facts to help us understand the time progression of Paul's journey to Rome. The return of the pronoun "we" marks the return of Luke as a traveling companion. A Roman citizen like Paul who appealed to the emperor would be treated better than most prisoners. Stopping at Sidon, Paul is allowed to visit his friends. The friends are part of a church that was probably established during the persecution that followed the death of Stephen (7:54-60).
Are there any older people in your church who you can talk to, to hear some stories about God's faithfulness? Be sure to take some notes. Can you relate to any of the stories? Will you ask God to give you some stories of your own in the future?

WEDNESDAY • Acts 27:14-29

DIGGING DEEPER Verse 14 describes a violent storm. "Euroclydon" was the name of the gust, meaning "east wind and north wind." It was a strong and dangerous wind and was greatly feared by those who sailed. This weather was part of God's purpose in getting Paul to Rome. In verse 18 the lightening of the ship is them throwing overboard all the unnecessary gear and cargo to let the ship ride higher on the waves. Paul encouraged the crew that not only would he appear before the emperor but that they all would survive for his sake.

Until we've fulfilled the purpose God has for us we are indestructible. Are there any situations ahead of you that scare you? How should you prepare yourself today?

THURSDAY • Acts 27:30-44

DIGGING DEEPER Look at the situation on this ship. Everyone is freaking out! Paul with the peace of knowing that nothing bad can happen to him helps them calm down. He tells them to stay on board so they can all stick together (v. 30) then to make sure they eat (v. 34). This was no small ship. Luke notes that there were 276 people on board (v. 37). God's guidance continues after the ship runs aground. This time He uses the centurion to keep the prisoners from being killed (vv. 42-43).

Are you ever in stressful situations in school or at your job? How can having a calm spirit show people you know Who is in control?

FRIDAY • Acts 28:1-16

DIGGING DEEPER Many times in our lives God changes our plans and we have to wait for Him. But He always expects us to keep serving even when plans change. Paul did just that for three months (v. 11) on the island of Malta. A poisonous snake bit Paul while he gathered sticks for a fire. Paul's survival was because of God's miraculous intervention. God used this incident to once again validate Paul as His messenger and use him as a testimony to the people around him. God uses Paul to do many miracles in the next few weeks to point them to Him.

Times of waiting aren't excuses to stop serving God! Even as He prepares you for future ministry can you find ways to be involved today? Where does your church need some help right now?

SATURDAY • Acts 28:17-31

DIGGING DEEPER Paul is put under house arrest but God keeps bringing people. These Jewish leaders hadn't heard the accusations against Paul and were at least willing to hear him out. Look at verses 26-27 which are quoting Isaiah. God knew hundreds of years before that even after He sent His Son to die and performed many miracles to show that the Gospel was true, the Jews would still not believe. Yet God kept sending His servants and Paul kept preaching. God always gives people a chance to believe. He is looking for a remnant to accept this truth.

Our job is not to look at the results—our job is to share the Word! Look at Paul's example in being faithful without dwelling on results. Who needs to hear from you today? Do you need to sketch out a plan of where you will go so you can be regularly sharing the Gospel?

WEEK 36

Have you ever wanted to talk to God face-to-face? This week you will read about two prophets who did. Habakkuk was brave enough to ask God why He wasn't doing anything about wicked people. Zephaniah got some bad news and some good news about God's coming judgment.

PRAYER FOCUS FOR THIS WEEK

THE QUESTION: What is the writer saying?

THE ANSWER: How can I apply this to my life?

SUNDAY • Habakkuk 1:1-11

DIGGING DEEPER Have you ever wanted to talk to God in person and ask Him questions about things that really bother you? We all have from time to time. That is what this little book is about. The prophet asks God how long he has to cry out and not be heard. He couldn't understand why God was not judging Judah for its obvious sins. Notice that God does not rebuke Habakkuk or tell him not to ask these questions. He answers him. God says He will be using an even more sinful nation to punish the people. That certainly doesn't seem right does it? But God had a specific plan for how all this would be used for His glory. Sin always has consequences, but because God is longsuffering those consequences do not always come immediately. **What questions do you have for God? He wants to hear them.**

MONDAY • Habakkuk 1:12–2:1

DIGGING DEEPER Have you ever wondered what God was doing in your life? Habakkuk was amazed at what he heard. How could God use these wicked Chaldeans to carry out His justice? How could He stand there silently and let wicked people devour righteous ones? Habakkuk seems to question the very character of God. How could a loving, righteous God allow this? It seemed to go against everything Habakkuk thought God was. Notice that as Habakkuk questions God, he doesn't do it out of personal selfishness. He doesn't ask why life isn't fair for him. He points to God and says, "This is what *You* said. Now, what's going on?"

Think about the questions you have for God. Are they rooted in your unhappiness or you not being content with what He has for you? How can you put your questions in light of Who He is?

TUESDAY • Habakkuk 2:2-14

DIGGING DEEPER God answers Habakkuk's questions and tells him to write the answers down so everyone can read them and be warned. God wanted a permanent record so that when it was fulfilled everyone would clearly understand. Fulfillment of prophecy can take time but you can be sure it will come true in God's appointed time (v. 3). Meanwhile God reminds Habakkuk, "The just shall live by faith" (v. 4). When we think of righteousness we usually think of commandments, Proverbs, or rules. But God doesn't want us checking off a list of good things! He says here that true righteousness is just trusting Him—even among evil people.

Do you ever get caught up in doing good things? Are there practical ways you can trust God today? Do you need God's help understanding His way of righteousness?

WEDNESDAY • Habakkuk 2:15-20

DIGGING DEEPER God lists two more reasons why the enemy will be punished. First, verses 15-17 tell us they were disgraceful and inhumane by getting their neighbor drunk in order to shame him. God says He will have divine retribution and repay them. Second, in verses 18-20 God looks at their greatest sin, idolatry. He asks what good their fake gods are. In contrast Habakkuk reminds us that "The Lord is in His holy temple." How wonderful it is to serve and worship a living, self-existent, eternal, holy God Who rules the universe. Compare these passages: Psalms 11:4; 18:6, 9; and Micah 1:2-3. This is where we should focus our lives.

Are you living your life believing that God is ultimately in control? Do you know in your heart that sin will be judged and righteousness will prevail?

THURSDAY • Habakkuk 3:1-19

DIGGING DEEPER This final chapter is Habakkuk's prayer of praise and worship. It shows that he is no longer focused on the circumstances but on God no matter what goes on around him. In verses 3-16 he reviews some of Israel's history. Habakkuk uses these events to form the background for God's future judgment on His enemies (v. 12) and the deliverance of His people (v. 13). The final three verses are Habakkuk's confession of faith. What Habakkuk is saying can be paraphrased, "Even though everything around me falls apart, I will rejoice in the God Who saved me. He gives me the strength I need to face the hard times ahead."

Even if Habakkuk is still having trouble trusting God he doesn't show it. He repeats what God has done and praises Him. How can you reflect on what God has done? How can you use this to help you trust Him today?

DIGGING DEEPER Have you ever had someone tell you he had good news and bad news and ask which you wanted first? This book gives the bad news first for Judah and the enemies of God's people. "God must judge sin" is the message of this book. The phrase "The Day of the Lord" occurs many times in Old Testament prophecy and can be understood in two main ways. First, it refers to the writer's present time when judgment is coming. Second, it speaks to the future time when God will bring eternal judgment. With such severe judgment in view the doomed were called together to seek repentance (2:1-3). God's people were judged more harshly because of the many blessings and warnings He had sent them.
Are you ready for the final "Day of the Lord"? If not, talk to someone who can help you. If so, tell a friend about Jesus so they can be ready.

SATURDAY • Zephaniah 3:8-20

DIGGING DEEPER Are you ready for some good news? The tone of the book changes here when Zephaniah gives a glimmer of hope by telling the people to wait on God. God was going to take action for them when they turn back to Him. In verses 19-20 Zephaniah describes the millennial age and some of the blessings that will come with it. There will be pure worship. The people there won't be full of sin, distrust, or trickery. They will be joyful and safe. Christ will rule over them and make all things right. How do we know this will happen? Verse 20 says God says so!
Look at the promises of verse 17. God promises great joy as He saves us— and that we will "rest in His love." Christ's salvation gives us a glimpse of this today, even before Heaven. Have you ever rested in God's love? Is this something you would like His help with today?

WEEK 37

On a trip have you ever asked your parents, "Are we there yet?" Moses is giving the final instructions to the Israelites after their 40-year trip through the wilderness. This week's quiet time is the start of our journey with Moses as he gets the children of Israel ready for their final steps into the Promised Land!

PRAYER FOCUS FOR THIS WEEK

THE QUESTION: What is the writer saying?

THE ANSWER: How can I apply this to my life?

SUNDAY • Deuteronomy 1:1-18

DIGGING DEEPER You thought family vacations were long! Can you imagine a 40-year trip and you aren't there yet even though you've been waiting around just a short distance away? Moses is giving final instructions to the people to go in and take the land that God promised to Abraham in Genesis 13:15. The Israelites' impatience had kept them from going straight into the Promised Land 40 years ago and he wanted to make sure it didn't happen again. This lesson is good for us too. We need to make sure no matter how excited we are to do God's work, that we are ready and listening to Him before we go.

Think about the different situations in life you may be ready to jump into—a new job, a new school year, or maybe a ministry opportunity. Have you spent time talking to God about it? Have you looked to His Word?

MONDAY • Deuteronomy 1:19-31

DIGGING DEEPER In this passage Moses brings up the failure that Israel had experienced nearly 40 years before. They had their chance at the land the first time they came to the Jordan but they complained and were afraid. Moses reminds the people about God's loving protection in their journey out of Egypt. God had carried them (v. 31) the whole way. It may seem harsh that a little grumbling had delayed for so long but God was pointing at a deeper heart attitude. The people wanted their way more than God's and that is what Moses is warning against here.

Even after God punishes us for a wrong attitude we often sin the same way again. What sins in your life do you continue to struggle with? How can you make yourself remember the consequences—or remember how God has been faithful and carried you?

TUESDAY • Deuteronomy 1:32-46

DIGGING DEEPER Moses continues his reminder to the people of why some of them can't enter the Promised Land. After not trusting God and being told "no" they tried to go in on their own (v. 41). The result was disaster and death. This failure made the Israelites even more sorry—they were ready to follow God now (v. 45)! But God wanted them to put Him first. He let them wallow in this sorrow in hopes that they would finally understand that *He* was God and they would stop trying to control their lives.

The next time you are feeling down about your sin take a minute to really think about your choices. Where do you need to let God be in control?

WEDNESDAY • Deuteronomy 2:14-18; 3:21-29

DIGGING DEEPER The 40 years of wilderness wandering (2:7) is broken into three parts. It took 13 months and 20 days to go from Egypt to Mt. Sinai, then 10 months to get to Kadesh-barnea, and then fail to enter the land. Now 38 years later the Israelites are finally approaching the border of the Promised Land again. All of the men of war (over 20 years of age) were on a death march. Their lives would end before Israel moved on. Notice that even Moses had to pay for his disobedience. Despite all his time serving God he would only get a glimpse of the Promised Land. He was a reminder that no matter how much we obey God and no matter how much He uses us, what God wants is total obedience.

God is serious about obedience! Are there any areas where you are being convicted to obey? How has God promised that He'll help you with this?

THURSDAY • Deuteronomy 4:1-10

DIGGING DEEPER Moses' words to Israel were coming after the terrible events of Numbers 25 where 24,000 people had died in a plague and judgment of God (4:3). Now Moses tells the people to obey exactly what God has told them to do. What other nation has God spoken to (v. 7)? What other nation has specific commandments to follow and obey (v. 8)? Moses tells them to take care of their souls (v. 9) so they don't forget what God taught them. These truths would be passed on from fathers to their children and grandchildren.

God knows we have a hard time remembering what He's shown and taught us. That's why He tells us to build habits into our lives to help us remember. How is your quiet time? Are you being refreshed each day?

FRIDAY • Deuteronomy 4:21-31

DIGGING DEEPER Have you ever made such a big mistake that all you wanted to do was warn others not to do it? Moses was talking to the younger generation of Israelites. They knew their parents were being punished but they hadn't personally experienced the same situation. Moses says, "Don't try this yourself! You've got to trust me." He points to two characteristics of God: (1) God is jealous (v. 24) meaning He won't let others have His honor. But if the Israelites do worship other gods or follow their selfishness, He's also (2) merciful (v. 31)—He's ready to forgive and get them back on the right track.

Is there anyone warning you about your actions that you should be listening to today? What if you've already messed up—are you looking to God for His mercy? He wants you to come back.

SATURDAY • Deuteronomy 4:32-40

DIGGING DEEPER Moses asks some rhetorical (self-answering) questions to make the Israelites reflect on their special status with God. No other nation had known God like Israel had or received such detailed instruction. Look at verse 39— Moses tells the people, "You've heard this before but think about it in your heart. Think about Who this God is." Often as Christians we just glaze over verses like this. "Yeah, God is great, mighty, wondrous, powerful, blah, blah." Take some time to slow down and really consider what this is saying about God.

Do you know this God in your personal life? What do you understand about all of these characteristics? They are worth more than mere casual consideration.

WEEK 38

What is the consuming passion of your life? Moses gets to the heart of obedience during this week's quiet time. To love God is the key for a lifetime of obedience. Moses walked with God like no other person in Israel. That is why he commanded the people with such clarity and power.

PRAYER FOCUS FOR THIS WEEK

THE QUESTION: What is the writer saying?

THE ANSWER: How can I apply this to my life?

SUNDAY • Deuteronomy 5:1-21

DIGGING DEEPER Did your parents or teachers ever say, "Hey, I'm talking to you?" This is what Moses says in verses 3-4. The commandments were given to these people's parents nearly 40 years before but they were meant for the present generation as well. God told the parents to teach these instructions to their children and the next generation was accountable for carrying them out just as if they had been there themselves. God's truth is the same for all people at all times and these ancient commandments are still true for us today.

God is talking to you. Are you listening? Take extra time today in your quiet time to write out the answer to "How can I apply this to my life?"

DIGGING DEEPER Moses was the mediator—he stood between man and God. This was not an easy job! The people saw the burning fire, heard the voice of God on the mountain, and saw the tablets of the Ten Commandments that Moses brought down. They needed someone to go and interact with God for them. Moses stood before God and faced possible death for them. This had happened nearly 40 years before but it was still fresh on Moses' mind. He wouldn't forget what it was like to get the instructions firsthand and he didn't want the people to forget it either. **How close do you want to be to God? Is just a little bit of God good enough for you or do you want to know Him deeply and personally? How serious are you about your walk with God today?**

DIGGING DEEPER Jesus quoted from Deuteronomy on many occasions as He showed how obeying God was still important even as He brought forgiveness. The Bible is clear that doing good doesn't save us in itself. But it does create space for God to work in us. Whether we are children, young Christians, or spiritually mature believers doing what's right continually keeps us in right standing with God, with our minds set on God so He can help us grow.

God puts a lot of emphasis on obeying commandments but we need to focus not on *what* we're obeying but *Who* we're obeying! Think about your motivation for doing right. Do you do it because you know you should or are you learning more about God and growing? Do you need to ask someone for help with this?

WEDNESDAY • Deuteronomy 6:12-25

DIGGING DEEPER "Massah" in verse 16 refers to testing and the events in Exodus 17:1-7. Moses uses this story of the striking of the rock in Horeb to remind the people not to argue with God. It was their complaining there and later in Numbers 20:7-13 that led to Moses' sin in striking the rock the second time when he was told to only speak to it. Moses knew all too well the consequences of disobedience and he spoke from a passionate heart when he told the people to keep these commandments and teach them to their children. Moses took responsibility for his actions as he encouraged others to watch out.

Are there any sins in your life that you are blaming on other people? Do you need to accept responsibility for them? Are there people in your life you can encourage to make the same choice?

THURSDAY • Deuteronomy 8:1-10

DIGGING DEEPER The physical needs of our life point to our greater spiritual need. With the Israelites God took care of their physical needs so they would focus on Him. He not only gave them plenty of food (v. 4) but also kept their clothes from wearing out and their bodies strong (v. 5). His future promise (vv. 7-10) was all about physical fulfillment.

Do you really believe that God is taking care of all your physical needs? Do you need to put more attention into making your spiritual needs come first?

DIGGING DEEPER It's all about God; it's not about you. Sometimes we look at all the blessings of God and forget that the reason He blesses us is so that we will know and worship Him. Moses knew that once the people crossed the Jordan River and settled in the Promised Land they would be tempted to forget God. We need to be careful not to be ruined by prosperity; it can lift us up in pride and cause us to forget God.

Do you ever find yourself wishing for just a little more money, some new clothes, or a nicer room? Could God be keeping you in this place so you'll remember to look to Him? How can you look for God today?

SATURDAY • Deuteronomy 9:1-12

DIGGING DEEPER What giants do you have in your life? What is so big that you cannot possibly defeat it without God's help? Moses tells the people that they will defeat the giants. Notice what else he says though—God isn't doing it because the people are so great (v. 4). We are merely tools for God or objects of His favor. We don't deserve prosperity or victory but He chooses to give it to us. When we align our will with God's He has a lot of room to work in our lives.

Do you have a giant sin or obstacle in your life? Why not ask God to defeat that giant?

How do you feel toward people who stick up for you? Moses went to God and begged Him not to destroy rebellious Israel. You will see the great heart of God as Moses pours out God's love and instruction to the people. This guidance would be for the blessing, prosperity, and literal survival of the nation.

PRAYER FOCUS FOR THIS WEEK

THE QUESTION: What is the writer saying?

THE ANSWER: How can I apply this to my life?

SUNDAY • Deuteronomy 9:13-29

DIGGING DEEPER Have you ever had a friend stick up for you when you really messed up? Maybe it was when you were younger and didn't realize what a serious mistake you made. The person who defended you was saying to the person in charge, "He's young and he's got no clue what a big deal this is but give him a break—God can still use him." That's what Moses does for the Israelites here. They were so clueless about how upsetting their behavior was to God. While Moses knew how sinful they were—and was even upset himself—he also knew God could work through them.

Can you remember when someone stuck up for you? Do you need to thank that person today? Is there someone you know who could use a second chance?

MONDAY • Deuteronomy 10:1-10

DIGGING DEEPER Despite the Israelites' sin God gave them another try at obeying Him. Notice how Moses carefully follows God's directions here. He had seen God forgive others and give second chances but he never focused on what had happened with those other people. He just kept his eyes on doing what was right. Moses had a pretty thankless job. He stuck up for sinners and was held to a high standard even as others disobeyed. But Moses also had the advantage of working with God personally. He knew God and relied on His strength.

Do you ever get discouraged doing God's work? What can you learn from Moses?

TUESDAY • Deuteronomy 10:11-22

DIGGING DEEPER Look at verse 12 as the specific instructions for the nation of Israel are given. These directions are the same for Christians today. First was to *fear* God—to have a proper idea of Who God is and respect the choices He makes and directions He gives. Second was to *walk* in His ways or to follow the instructions He had given that showed how people should live if they were reflecting His character. Next, the Israelites were to *love* God. This wasn't supposed to be a list of rules or an authoritarian regime. God wanted a relationship with these people. Finally, God told the people to *serve* Him with everything they had.

Can you think of any New Testament verses that teach these same principles? With which of these do you struggle?

DIGGING DEEPER Notice that today's passage has love coming before obedience. The people of Israel when they started complaining and disobeying usually did it because they were not anchored in a loving relationship with God. They focused on the blessings He would give them or the rules He would hand down, not on what it was like to seek Him. Because He had saved them so many times they knew to follow Him but He warned of a time when their children wouldn't know about these great events. He wants to make sure they taught the next generation to follow Him.

Do you ever forget the great things God has done for you? Do you ever focus on what He's giving you or His instructions rather than getting to know Him? What should you do?

DIGGING DEEPER Did your parents ever tell you that if you didn't behave you wouldn't get dessert? It wasn't as nice as you just obeying but it sure worked! Unfortunately that's what God had to do with Israel too. He linked their physical blessings with their spiritual behavior until they could "grow up" and just obey Him on their own! In verses 26-32 God's message is the same, but this time it is presented in the "blessing/curse" format. God was using different renditions of the same message to say "obey."

Are there any areas in your life where you know you should be obedient but are waiting for God to reward you first? Do you need His help with obeying without necessarily seeing the results?

DIGGING DEEPER Moses continued to share God's plans for success and survival with the children of Israel. Chapters 12-14 cover warnings against idol worship, following false prophets, tithing, and what food to eat. Chapter 15 discusses poverty and social justice. A wealthy Israelite could take a fellow Israelite into his home to pay a debt and make him a slave but only for six years. When seven years were completed, he was set free with enough provisions to get back on his feet. Some out of love for their masters would willingly decide to stay and become lifelong servants.

Do you consider yourself to be a bondservant of Jesus Christ? Consider Philemon 1, James 1:1, 2 Peter 1:1, and Jude 1. Have you decided to be a lifelong follower of Jesus Christ willingly and submit to Him out of love?

SATURDAY • Deuteronomy 16:1-17

DIGGING DEEPER Moses tells the people of Israel about the three "pilgrim" holidays they are to observe. These all required a trip to the Tabernacle. The first holiday ("holy day") is the Passover (vv. 1-8) which was in the spring (around the month of March). This was the start of the Jewish calendar. The Passover reminded the people of the death of the firstborns of Egypt and how the angel passed over them sparing them. The sign of the blood on the door frames foreshadowed Christ our Passover lamb (1 Corinthians 5:7) Who was sacrificed for the sin of the whole world. The feast of weeks is Pentecost 50 days later in May/June (vv. 9-12). Then came the Feast of Tabernacles in verses 13-15 (Zechariah 14).

The Israelites had special events mandated so they'd remember what God had done. How do you reflect regularly on what God has done in your life?

WEEK 40

This book and the life of Moses is ending fast. Moses finishes his life on earth with a great testimony. Except for the few missteps mentioned in Scripture he finishes his life passionately walking with God. Look for a few surprises along the way as we finish this great book this week.

PRAYER FOCUS FOR THIS WEEK

THE QUESTION: What is the writer saying?

THE ANSWER: How can I apply this to my life?

SUNDAY • Deuteronomy 18:9-22

DIGGING DEEPER Deuteronomy 16:18 – 18:8 gives instructions for judges, how to bring offerings, what to do with idol worshipers, how to behave towards authority, how to choose a king, and how to care for priests. In today's passage verses 9-14 show us how to handle satanic practices. Verses 15-19 were used by Christ in John 5:46-47 and Peter declared that Jesus was the Messiah based on these verses in his second sermon in Acts 3:22-23.

Do you see Jesus in these verses? God told kings to have a copy of the Bible with them in the throne room at all times (Deuteronomy 17:18-20) so they could stay fresh in the promises of God. What does this tell you about the importance of the Bible in your life?

DIGGING DEEPER In chapters 19-29 God gives many specific instructions for how Jewish society was supposed to function. Scholars have figured out some of the reasoning behind these laws—for example, some of the restrictions had health benefits for people living in that time of history. But the main focus was that Israel was set apart for God, and its people would trust that God knew best in everything He was telling them to do, whether they could see it or not.

There are a lot of things that Christians do that other people don't understand. But people sure know what a Christian looks like! How can you use these things to point people toward obeying God?

DIGGING DEEPER In verse 19 Moses' words go a level deeper. He's saying, "I know what you're thinking. You're smiling and nodding now, but you're already thinking of ways you can pretend you're following God while you do what you want. He's not fooled! He'll know." Notice that the punishment would not only affect the person sinning but would also spread to that person's family. The consequences of our sin naturally affect others but our encouragement can also push those around us toward good!

Can you think of how your actions have affected those around you recently? Is there anything you're trying to hide in your heart that God already knows about? What should you do?

WEDNESDAY • Deuteronomy 30:1-14

DIGGING DEEPER Moses has been going on and on about how, if the Israelites will follow God good stuff will happen. Yet in these verses he starts talking about captivity. God obviously didn't have high hopes that they'd always obey! Moses reiterates that the instructions are easy and obvious (vv. 11-14). As he describes what the people have to look forward to Moses describes many of the same promises Christians have been given. The human life is the story of our journey back to God. **Romans 5:8 says that God saved us "when we were yet sinners"—He knew we would mess up! Do you need to do any turning back to God? What is waiting for you if you do?**

THURSDAY • Deuteronomy 31:1-13

DIGGING DEEPER Moses is 120 years old and now ready to pass off the baton of leadership to Joshua. Joshua who God had chosen to lead the people into the Promised Land had proven his ability for many years. He commanded the Israelite army (Exodus 17:9). He went up Mt. Sinai with Moses (Exodus 24:13). He and Caleb made the right choice at Kadesh-barnea (Numbers 26:65). God confirmed him as the next leader in Numbers 27:17-18. Moses (vv. 6-7) uses the same words God uses in Joshua 1:6-9. Joshua doesn't have to fear because he's God's choice. **Joshua served God faithfully for many years before this decision was made. Looking at the verses describing him what sticks out to you about Joshua? What part of Joshua's example do you want to follow?**

FRIDAY • Deuteronomy 32:1-14

DIGGING DEEPER These are the words of someone who has personally known God. It's easy to gloss over them because we see phrases like this in the Bible all the time, but try to take a minute and see what they really mean. What does it mean to say God is a rock—or *the* Rock (v. 4)? What is perfection (v. 4)? Look at the picture in verse 11—how much did God love Israel?

Do you need help getting a fresh picture of how great God is? Who can you go to for help with learning about Him? Will you take time to write your own description of God today?

SATURDAY • Deuteronomy 34:1-12

DIGGING DEEPER Moses is at the end of his life so let's take a minute to remember where he came from. He had been born in Egypt and brought up completely separate from the people of Israel. God slowly pulled him toward Him showing Moses Who He was and what His plan was for Israel. They were in the wilderness together as God trained Moses to be a great leader. Moses would stand before Pharaoh, take a nation across the desert, and be led by God's personal touch, all the while telling him about this great land at the end of the trip. Now Moses finally got to see it. Notice that verse 7 says he was still healthy and still respected by all the people he had rebuked so many times (v. 8)!

What will your legacy be? Are you living in such a way that people will mourn for you and always remember you as a man or woman who walked with God?

WEEK 41

Have you ever asked God why something bad was happening to you? We'll see this week that Job did. You know the story of his loss and suffering but dig deeper this week to discover God's sovereignty and power over life and death. Learn how to be a true friend to someone who is hurting.

PRAYER FOCUS FOR THIS WEEK

THE QUESTION: What is the writer saying?

THE ANSWER: How can I apply this to my life?

SUNDAY • Job 1:1-12

DIGGING DEEPER What do you think about when you think of Job? Most people remember his suffering and trials. Let's turn it around and ask, "Is God worth trusting when everything in life goes wrong?" Job was a very blessed man but notice that God also calls him "blameless" and "upright." When Satan heard that he said it was because God had given Job everything. But if God took it away Satan thought Job would change his tune. Satan could not believe that anyone would follow God simply for Who He was not for what He gives. As we read on we see that God allowed Satan to take his possessions but not to touch his body. It is important for us to realize that what happened to Job was not a result of sin.
Would God call you "blameless"? Is there anything you need to trust Him with today—focusing on Him and not whether He's blessing you?

MONDAY • Job 1:13-22

DIGGING DEEPER When you hear bad news what is the first thing you do? Worship God? Probably not! We all experience loss in our lives but few of us ever have the extreme Job did. When the first messenger came it's easy to imagine Job being sad for the loss of a vital part of his business but more concerned for the families of his slain servants. Then the second and third servants arrived with their horrible news. His livelihood was totally destroyed; all of his income was gone. Then the fourth messenger came with news of the death of all ten of his children. Imagine the sorrow Job and his wife must have felt. Notice that Job fell down and worshiped God. Even in his loss he knew he could still trust God.
God may allow hard things to happen to you but we can trust that He also has a reason. Do you need to worship Him today?

TUESDAY • Job 2:1-13

DIGGING DEEPER Are there people in your life who are hard to please? It seems like they are not satisfied with anything. That is the way Satan is with God about Job. God allowed him to take everything away from Job but Job still had his health. So Satan wanted that too, thinking Job would finally turn his back on God. God told Satan he could touch Job physically but he could not kill him. This proves that God is in charge of life and death. Notice how severely Job is afflicted with physical problems. He hurts from head to toe and looks to be alone sitting in ashes. He does have three loyal friends who come and sit quietly with him for a week.
Who is in control of your life and death? Praise and worship God for Who He is. Is there a friend you need to sit with and comfort? List a few friends that could use your help.

DIGGING DEEPER What is the best way to help a friend after he has experienced a loss? Most of the time it is best to just be there and let him talk. In chapters 4-5 Job's friends challenged him to get right with God. They mistakenly thought that there was unconfessed sin in his life and that he was being punished by God which chapter one says was not true. Job is replying to them as well as to God here. We sense his frustration and the hurt he feels. We also see how intense his physical suffering has become. It is not wrong for us to ask God why something has happened but it is important that we are asking with a heart that is open to learn. **Is there a friend you need to comfort? Be there for them without assuming. Is there a** *why* **question you have for God? Go ahead and ask Him.**

THURSDAY • Job 9:1-20

DIGGING DEEPER In chapter eight Job's friend, Bildad, tells him that God is just so Job must have done something to deserve this punishment. Job says he knows perfectly well that God is just and that all men are sinners. He also says that God can do whatever He wants with His creation. Job's affirming God's character again shows that he did not have a sinful attitude. Still despite his trust, Job feels like God is crushing him and there is nothing he can do to stop it. He wonders if God is even listening. In verses 17-18 we see that this is really getting to him and that he's getting a bad attitude. We also see that no matter how mature you are in God when you face suffering and loss things can get out of perspective. **Do you struggle with remembering the truth about God when hard times come? How can you remind yourself today of Who He is?**

FRIDAY • Job 9:21-35

DIGGING DEEPER Do you know any hypocrites—people who pretend to be something they're not? That's what Job's friends were accusing him of and we see Job struggling with it. Job knew there was no unconfessed sin in his life but after two of his friends said over and over that he must be hiding sin Job began to weaken. Job realizes how short life is comparing it to both a sprint runner and an eagle swooping down to eat its prey. Both are really fast! Verses 27-28 show that Job was a man of integrity. He refused to act like nothing was wrong when he was in such turmoil. He knew he could make himself look good on the outside for his friends but that would not solve his problem.

What can we learn from Job's honesty and humility in the face of untrue accusations?

SATURDAY • Job 10:1-2, 8-22

DIGGING DEEPER Have you ever wondered why God allowed some things to happen in your life? Job sure did. He knew that God was sovereign and nothing happened without His permission. Although Job did not know God was using this he was determined to follow God simply for Who He was. Job also wondered why God would create him just to destroy him. His frustration got to the point where he said it would be better if he'd never been born. When people are hurting they need to be assured that there is a loving and caring God who will work all things out for good (Romans 8:28).

While we know God is using all for good sometimes we try to figure out exactly why each time. But that can lead to worrying or us not really trusting Him. In what new ways can you learn to trust God?

WEEK 42

How many really close friends do you have—friends who will stick with you no matter what happens? This week we'll see that Job's "friends" were not a big help to him. In fact they made things worse. Watch as Job clings to God knowing that He knows everything and will make things right.

PRAYER FOCUS FOR THIS WEEK

THE QUESTION: What is the writer saying?

THE ANSWER: How can I apply this to my life?

SUNDAY • Job 12:1-4, 13-25

DIGGING DEEPER Have you ever had people misunderstand and judge you wrongly? Sometimes even our closest friends don't understand what we're going through. In chapter 11 Job's friend, Zophar, begs Job to repent saying his sin was the reason for what was happening to him. Job acknowledges that his friend has wisdom but says he has some understanding about the situation too. He says he is clean before God. They don't believe him. In verses 13-25 we see Job begin to rest in the character of God. He and his friends could at least agree that God was ultimately in control. With nothing else left Job let God take care of him.

People will always want to tell us what we should be doing but we must look at God's standards to see if we're living right. Can you rest in God's sovereignty today? Do you need to learn more about Him first?

MONDAY • Job 13:1-18

DIGGING DEEPER Job and his friends continue their struggle. Job knew he was right even if he didn't have much of a way to prove it. He insists that his suffering was not the judgment of God as his friends claimed. He begged them to be fair when listening to him. In verse 13 Job tells them to just be quiet and listen to him because he knew God would show them he was right; he knew he was telling the truth. Job's trust in God had nothing to do with what was happening in his life. His trust was based on Who he knew God to be.

Job had no defense except what he knew was true about God. How should you react when people question your views? Do you have the kind of relationship with God where you can tell people with assurance that you're right before Him?

TUESDAY • Job 14:1-15

DIGGING DEEPER Job starts talking about how short and fragile life is. Life can disappear so fast Job says and it sometimes seems controlled by chance. God is the One however, Who controls how long we live (v. 5). Job was concerned with having the approval of God and learning how God worked in the world—especially His plans for people (vv. 10-15). When we think about life it can sometimes be confusing. It's easier to not ask the tough questions. But Job pushed deeper knowing that only God knows the answers.

Do you take time to think about the difficult questions of life? Or do you shy away from them because they make you uncomfortable, or you think you can't figure out the answers? Can you think of one question you should explore today?

WEDNESDAY • Job 16:1-22

DIGGING DEEPER What is the best thing to do for a friend who is hurting? Don't follow Job's friends' example! In chapter 15 Eliphaz told Job that he was being foolish, was dodging the issues, and was a hypocrite. This chapter is Job's response. Remember he is in incredible pain, he can't sleep, his skin is falling off, and he aches all over. And his friends are calling him a liar! Job tells them they are doing nothing to relieve his grief (v. 6). Instead of helping they are making things worse (v. 8). Through his tears he could still pray confident that God heard him even if his friends didn't. In verse 21 Job is looking for someone to care enough about him to pray with and for him not to judge him or try to explain what was happening.

Do you ever try to solve someone's problems for them when they just need love and support? Can you make this right today?

THURSDAY • Job 17:1-16

DIGGING DEEPER Who do you go to when you need advice? It is important to go to people who love and follow God and as a result love you. Job is still struggling between knowing he is right with God and his friends' unhelpful attitudes. One lesson we learn in Scripture is that God is not the author of confusion. His truth is simple and if we seek Him all the other views that contradict Him will fall away. If you, like Job get counsel that leaves you confused take it to God to see whether it is the right application of Scripture for your struggle. Ask Him to direct your judgment. Take time to rest in God and see what He shows you.

People want to be helpful when we are hurting but the Holy Spirit is the One Who makes sure God's Word is being used the right way. Do you need to seek the Holy Spirit's guidance for a situation you're in right now?

FRIDAY • Job 19:19-29

DIGGING DEEPER When people know something is right or they're trying to prove a point they often put it in writing. They want to be able to come back and say, "See! I said it then and it came true." That has a lot more validity than a verbal "I told you so." Job is showing his faith in God in verses 23-27 as he wishes there was a way his account could be written down. He *knew* God would prove He was faithful and He wanted everyone to know Who He was. Job's friends and even Satan were focused on his physical death, but Job—as much as he was suffering—didn't fear that! He believed he would live again and finally get to see God in person.

Have you ever written down your struggles and how God has helped you so you can look back on or help others with your records of God's faithfulness?

SATURDAY • Job 23:1-12

DIGGING DEEPER Job, on top of all his physical problems is also having trouble talking to God. He doesn't know where to find Him but he knew if he could just get there they could talk the whole situation out (vv. 4-5). He just wants to know what's going on and he knows that being around God would give him strength (v. 6). Even though we sometimes think it would be better if we just understood, God has other ways of teaching us. Job knew this too, and although he wanted personal interaction with God he was still obedient. He repeated God's promises (v. 10) and followed His instructions (v. 11).

Do you still follow God even when it seems like He's not there? Do you obey even when you want answers?

WEEK 43

What do you do when you've done everything you know you should do and still don't understand what's going on? How do you get wisdom and understanding? What do you think God's answers to these questions would be? This week we'll learn the answers to these questions and more with Job and his friends.

PRAYER FOCUS FOR THIS WEEK

THE QUESTION: What is the writer saying?

THE ANSWER: How can I apply this to my life?

SUNDAY • Job 26:1-14

DIGGING DEEPER When you don't know what else to do what do you do? The best and only thing to do is totally trust God. That is what Job is doing in our passage today. His friends have been no comfort to him so he turns his focus to God and Who He is. We see that Job meditated on the majesty of God, His creativity, His sustaining power, and His just judgment. It's easy to see that Job had an intimate relationship with God before his trials began and could draw strength from Him in his time of deep need and sorrow.

How much time do you spend thinking about Who God really is? Do you reflect on Scripture and ask God to show you new things about Him? Take some of the things you've "always known" about God—such as His power or majesty—and ask yourself what that really looks like.

DIGGING DEEPER What is the most important thing to get in life? The Bible says wisdom. Today we see Job's concept of wisdom as he shares it with his friends. Wisdom is not found in the natural realm and it cannot be bought. It is more valuable than gold. Wisdom is eternal and more valuable than anything on earth. Job says that wisdom is only found in God. God will give wisdom to those who diligently seek Him (James 1:5). Job sums it up for us in the last verse. The fear of God equals wisdom and true understanding comes from departing from evil. To fear God doesn't mean to be afraid of Him as much as to be in awe of Him.

Wisdom takes knowledge and practically applies it to life taking basic information and turning it into God-like living. Where in your life would you like to see more wisdom today?

TUESDAY • Job 32:1-16

DIGGING DEEPER Have you ever listened to an older more mature person and not agreed with what he said? Job used chapters 29-31 to define his defense and point out that he had lived honorably before God. He still didn't think God was judging sin in his life. Elihu was a young man who had listened patiently and was upset with his friends for their quick condemnation of Job. Yet he was also upset with Job for almost charging God with doing wrong. We see Elihu had great respect for the older men; however, just because they were older didn't mean they had to be right in this situation. Elihu considered what they said and compared it with God's Word.

Can you think of a situation where an older person was wrong in their instructions? What is the right way to respond?

DIGGING DEEPER Have you ever been so excited to say something that it was hard to wait for the other person to finish? Elihu had listened patiently and was now going to tell these men what he thought. He explains his respect for them then warns that his motive was to tell the truth not to flatter them (v. 21). He explains that he's speaking from the heart and sharing knowledge from God. He wants Job to know that they were both created by God and that neither man is superior to the other. His careful and sensitive message to Job is that God is totally just and good.
It can be really hard to confront someone lovingly but Elihu gives a good example by explaining where he's coming from and treating these men with respect. How do you want to be treated when you're struggling? Can you think of practical ways to be loving to others when confronting them?

THURSDAY • Job 38:1-18

DIGGING DEEPER After all this time of waiting, of wanting to know where God was and trying to talk to Him, Job finally gets his chance. God answers Job by asking 50 questions of His own over the next three chapters. Each is designed for Job to realize God's greatness and to acknowledge that although Job didn't know why God allowed what He did He could be trusted. God asked Job Who created the natural order of the earth and if he understood the mysteries of how the universe works. God invited Job's questions and gave him one answer to consider: Himself. He wanted Job to think even more about Who He was.
When we ask questions it's from a human perspective. God's answer is to look at life from His point of view. What part of today's passage gives you a better idea of Who God is?

DIGGING DEEPER Job's story shows us that even a human living an almost completely righteous life has no idea of how in control God is. God says it's not right to look at life through human eyes. By earthly standards God seemed to be unfair. Job was not getting what he deserved. But God's idea of fairness and what He wants us to be is different. God is above earthly perspectives and wants to show us that we don't have to be tied down by man-made ideas when life can be so much better. **Do you ever find yourself trying to hold God to an earthly standard? Are you willing to try to see things from His point of view? Who can you ask to help you with this?**

SATURDAY • Job 42:1-17

DIGGING DEEPER What is going on in your life that you don't understand? Job says that as long as God knows, we're fine. Job tells God that he gets it, that God can do whatever He wants. He doesn't answer to anyone for it. Job repents for not trusting in the goodness and justice of God. God also deals with Job's three friends who hadn't spoken rightly about Him. Do you notice that God never told Job why He had allowed the trial? *We* understand after reading the first two chapters, but God didn't see the need to explain Himself. Job was trusting God because He was God, not so he could figure out life. **Do you get it? What are you trusting when you don't understand what's going on around you?**

WEEK 44

If there's ever a passage of Scripture you don't want to miss this is it! Are you really walking with Christ each day? What do you do if you're not? What keeps you from walking with Him? How do you know your friends are walking with Him? No matter who you are, this week is crucial! Dive in with all you've got!

PRAYER FOCUS FOR THIS WEEK

THE QUESTION: What is the writer saying?
THE ANSWER: How can I apply this to my life?

SUNDAY • 1 John 1:1-4

DIGGING DEEPER Ever wonder if you're really walking with Christ? Are you living the Christian life like God wants you to? Just about every believer wonders at some point. John tells us that this is actually why he wrote this book. You can have fellowship with Christ and you can be certain about it. And who would know better about friendship with Christ than someone who saw Him, touched Him, and walked with Him for three years on earth? That was John. The Gospels even tell us that, of all the disciples, John was the closest to Christ. John lets us know there is joy in walking with Christ and we can have a personal relationship with the very Son of God each day.

Do you have joy in your relationship with Christ? Why or why not? Will you commit to learning about walking in fellowship with Him?

MONDAY • 1 John 1:5-10

DIGGING DEEPER How does a Christian handle sin? That is the first basic topic John talks about. When it comes to walking with Christ day by day sin gets in the way. We can't ignore it. We all sin and God already knows about it so we should just tell Him about it. Verse 6 says we lie when we don't admit our own sin. Verse 9 tells us that when we admit sin to God He takes it from there. He will cleanse us so we can be back in a right relationship with Him. Sin is part of being human but God has given Christians a way to deal with it.

Is there any sin in your life that you have not admitted or confessed to God? Why not confess it?

TUESDAY • 1 John 2:1-6

DIGGING DEEPER Now that we know there is a way to take care of our sin it doesn't mean we do what we want and just confess it later. John's point in writing was so that we *wouldn't* sin (v. 1). Just in case you don't feel forgiven remember Who speaks on your behalf: Jesus Christ Himself (v. 2)! Since sin is still part of everyone's life John next looks at what makes a saved person different. Verses 3-6 say we should want to obey God's instructions. God knows we're not perfect but a genuine Christian will be working on pursuing Christ more than anything else.

If we focus on not sinning the Christian life can be a real struggle. But as we focus on Christ He works in us to make us more like Him. How often do you "keep His commandments" (v. 3)? Do you need help with obeying God?

WEDNESDAY • 1 John 2:7-11

DIGGING DEEPER So what's up with the "old" and "new" commandments? The command to love each other isn't new. These Christians in 1 John knew that. What was new about it was that Christ was the One giving the power. Believers now knew what perfect love was because Christ's death showed it to everyone (2:2). Verses 9-11 give one of those commands John was talking about in verse 3: You can't walk with Christ and not love other believers. Verse 11 gives some insight to a Christian who doesn't love. He's blind! While disobedience is one sign we aren't really following God, not having love for other people is another big one. The same love we have with God bleeds out into our relationship with others.
Ask yourself honestly: How much do you love others? Is this an area where you need God's help?

THURSDAY • 1 John 2:12-17

DIGGING DEEPER Verses 12-14 identify three different levels of Christians: "little children"—recently saved; "young men"—those saved for awhile and moving on to spiritual maturity; and "fathers"—aged and mature Christians who have been through the other stages. John uses these levels to remind the people that not all believers are at the same place in their Christian walks. It takes time to grow. For a good place to start John goes back to the idea of love. We know we're supposed to love God and others but he adds a couple things not to love here too: the world and its temporary pleasures.
Even if you are struggling with loving others you can start by not loving the things our human nature is drawn to in this world. Can you think of some things you shouldn't be loving? Who can you ask for help with this?

FRIDAY • 1 John 2:18-22

DIGGING DEEPER A lot of people call themselves Christians. We can tell the difference. The "antichrists" John is referring to here are those who weren't saved and were stirring up trouble in the church. They pretended to be Christians but didn't follow Christ's commands, didn't love fellow Christians, and loved the world. Genuine Christians have the Holy Spirit living inside of them Who helps them discern between truth and error.

Many non-Christians try to present an "easy way out"—they say we can still love the world or not follow God's directions. What should our response to them be?

SATURDAY • 1 John 2:23-27

DIGGING DEEPER John points out the importance of Christ and believing what we know is true about Him. He encourages the believers to both reflect on the doctrine they've been taught and know is true and to also continue in fellowship with each other going over the truth. Staying connected with Christ is the key to the Christian life. John encourages believers to stay away from false teachers and just stick to what they know is right.

What are you doing to learn more about Christ? What are you going to do to know Christ better? Who could help you know Him more?

WEEK 45

This week could be summed up in one word: *love*. There are many different ways God's love should influence us including our relationships with others and with God. If you get a handle on His love then you are guaranteed to walk with God like never before!

PRAYER FOCUS FOR THIS WEEK

THE QUESTION: What is the writer saying?
THE ANSWER: How can I apply this to my life?

SUNDAY • 1 John 2:28 - 3:3

DIGGING DEEPER With all this talk about what makes a Christian, how we should love, and that we shouldn't sin, we can sometimes get discouraged. It's really hard to follow God all the time! It's hard to love people! Even when Christ is working in us it takes a long time. But John says we should have confidence (v. 28). We don't have to worry about whether we're measuring up. God is doing the work and it starts with His intense love for us (v. 1). He has started the process and although we're only getting glimpses of how He is changing us (v. 2) we know that someday we're going to actually see Christ and finally be completely changed. That's why we keep trying (v. 3).

If Christ returned right now would He be pleased with your life? What can you do to honor Him? What should you stop doing?

MONDAY • 1 John 3:4-10

DIGGING DEEPER John says that people who obey God are the children of God and people who constantly sin are not. So what if the same sin keeps tripping you up? Does that mean you're not a child of God? Not necessarily. John does clarify that a genuine Christian does not *continue in sin*. Someone who really knows Christ will eventually turn around. The question for us is this: "Does my life characterize sin—or godly living?" The false teachers John warns about were unmistakably characterized by sinful, selfish living. John says, "Just look at their lives." We don't decide who is saved and who isn't but we do know how to spot someone who loves God versus someone who loves this world.

What would your parents, brothers, or sisters say about you? Do people think of you as a godly Christian?

TUESDAY • 1 John 3:11-16

DIGGING DEEPER John comes back to the idea of love again—and it's a good thing he does! As Christians we hear so much about love but often don't know what it practically looks like in life. The example here is Cain and Abel. Cain represents the original sinful human nature. Knowing he couldn't be righteous he got angry at his brother and killed him. In contrast Jesus—the epitome of righteousness—let Himself be killed so we could actually have that righteousness. He gives us a chance at a new nature that loves. By choosing to love we continue the process from the death of the old nature to the life of new rather than spreading hurt.

People who don't understand righteousness will often be unloving. Sometimes the best way to love them is by not reacting to the hurt they show us. Can you think of somewhere you should do this today?

WEDNESDAY • 1 John 3:17-24

DIGGING DEEPER Love isn't as hard as we think—sometimes it's as easy as seeing someone who needs something and giving it to him. John says it's not a philosophical concept or phrase we repeat (v. 18)—it's an action! The root of love and being aware of people's needs is the heart. God will work and give us confidence that the things we are doing are loving to others (vv. 20-21).

Are there opportunities around you to love people in helpful, practical ways? What excuses have you made to not help so far? What do these verses say about what happens to your relationship with God when you make an effort to love?

THURSDAY • 1 John 4:1-6

DIGGING DEEPER There are many ideas today that describe how to get to Heaven and Who Jesus is. How do you know who's right? That's what "test" or "try the spirits" (v. 1) means. 2 Peter 1:21 teaches that the Spirit of God wrote the Bible through men. So the way you know whether someone is telling the truth is whether what they say and do agrees with the Bible. That even includes your pastor or Sunday School teacher! Does it line up with all that the Bible says? Verse 4 reminds us that although this may sometimes seem difficult God is greater than anything Satan could try to confuse us with. We've got His perfect Word and it's never wrong.

Have you ever questioned what someone was teaching you? Did you go check it out in the Bible? Who can help you understand God's Word?

FRIDAY • 1 John 4:7-12

DIGGING DEEPER Have you ever bought an off-brand product that was made to look like the original? Maybe you wanted an authentic watch but one with different colors or lettering was cheaper. It may have worked OK but it was nothing like having the real thing. In today's passage we learn that the world has a lot of different definitions for love, but true love starts with God. Everything else—"love" for pizza, two people "loving" each other, the "love" for a sports team, even true human "love"—is just an imitation. Just like you'd rather have a watch that is guaranteed to work God wants you to have His perfect version of love.

Expert watchmakers can find signs of authenticity. What do these verses say are signs of God's love? How is this different from the way people try to love today?

SATURDAY • 1 John 4:13-21

DIGGING DEEPER When we come to Christ God starts the process of using the Holy Spirit to change us and make us more like Him. He takes us from our human nature, which has a cheap imitation of love, to His perfect version of love. The more He changes us the more that love comes out of us and is spread to others. Notice some signs of this love: boldness (v. 17), Christ-like living toward the world (v. 17), lack of fear (v. 18), perfection (v. 18), and truthfulness (v. 20). Once again the ultimate test in knowing whether we have God's love is how we treat others (v. 20). This is when we know God is working.

Which of these signs of love sticks out to you? Why is it important that God—and not something earthly—is the source of love?

WEEK 46

John had great love for the people to whom he was writing. As we finish 1 John and move to 2 John and 3 John we will see that the letters were addressed to different people. All sorts of difficult problems are addressed; many of them the same problems we deal with all the time. These are short but powerful letters!

PRAYER FOCUS FOR THIS WEEK

THE QUESTION: What is the writer saying?

THE ANSWER: How can I apply this to my life?

SUNDAY • 1 John 5:1-8

DIGGING DEEPER John continues his three main thoughts: loving God, loving fellow believers, and obeying God's commandments. All three must be true of us. If we are neglecting any one of them we are disobeying the other two as well. John goes one step further though. This is not only how to walk with God but also how we overcome the world. We have challenges, hard times, bullies, and all sorts of obstacles to deal with, but here's the key. We need to walk with God, stay in fellowship with Him each day, and confess our sin. When we focus on our relationship with Christ first He will take care of the rest. That's how we overcome the world!

What is difficult in your life right now? Will you give it to God and just focus on walking with Him today? Will you commit to not worrying?

MONDAY • 1 John 5:9-15

DIGGING DEEPER Ever feel you can't do anything right? Maybe you are discouraged about sports, music, school, or work? God wants you to have confidence but He wants that confidence to be in Him first (v. 13). John also gives instructions about prayer. We can have confidence that God hears us and will give us exactly what we need. That's the key—what we *need*. We need to be willing to submit to what He wants for us.
What situation do you need to pray about right now? Are you willing to submit to God's answer for you?

TUESDAY • 1 John 5:16-21

DIGGING DEEPER Verses 16-17 speak of two sins one of which leads to physical death. This sin refers to when a Christian repeatedly sins without remorse and can no longer be pulled back to God. At that time God takes him home. In this situation the Christian has clearly shown that his heart won't change and God considers his work on earth done. After sharing this tough news John reiterates that not all sin is like this. Some of it is part of the growing pains he talked about in chapter 1—it just needs to be confessed. As he closes the book after repeating his themes over and over John gives his instruction one more time with different phrasing. "Idols" would be anything that keeps us from God and His love.
Is there a sinning brother or sister in Christ for whom you should be praying? Is there sin in your life that you need to confess to God?

DIGGING DEEPER The "lady" in this book is most likely a person who had a church meeting in her house. John knew her and was pleased to see her children obeying God. This letter was probably addressed to a different church than 1 John was. That's why John starts off talking about the same things he did in the previous book—that we should love one another and obey God's Word. John is living these words as he writes his letter showing how much he cares for this woman and her children. John was concerned about the Christians in that area so he gave them a warning in hopes of protecting them.

To what Christian friend could you reach out today? What is the best way for you to be an encouragement to him?

THURSDAY • 2 John 7-13

DIGGING DEEPER This woman had teachers come into her home to teach the believers. John warned her about the false teachers in the area. He gave her some ways she could separate who was preaching the truth and who she shouldn't let inside her door. Although the church was young false teaching was already rampant. Some people were teaching that Jesus hadn't actually been a man (v. 7). John says it's no use arguing with these people—just turn them away (v. 10).

An easy way to recognize false teaching is to really know the truth. How often do you learn about doctrine and how it fits with your relationship with God? Who can help you with this today?

FRIDAY • 3 John 1-8

DIGGING DEEPER As John starts a new letter we see the special relationship he had with followers of Christ. Like a spiritual parent he wanted the best for God's children (v. 2). He was happy to hear that they were sticking to the truth (v. 3). He knew that was the basis for their Christian walk. In verses 5-8 he starts talking about the point of the letter. He affirms that it was good that Gaius and others were showing hospitality.

Is there anyone you can encourage in his spiritual walk? Sometimes people need to know they're on the right track. Whom can you encourage today?

SATURDAY • 3 John 9-14

DIGGING DEEPER John gets to the problem here. While Gaius had been faithfully following God, others in the church were not living in love and truth. One man, Diotrephes, always wanted to be first. He spread bad rumors about John. He kicked out the faithful brothers whom John had sent as well as those who disagreed with him. That's what Gaius had to deal with. John reminded Gaius not to be frustrated or try to fight Diotrephes—not to do the same thing Diotrephes was doing causing a power struggle in the church. John was coming soon and he would handle it. It's easy to think it's fair to return evil for evil but John encouraged Gaius to always do good.

Have you done something wrong because someone did it to you first? How can you prepare yourself to do right to those who treat you badly?

WEEK 47

Have you ever been a part of a church that seemed like one big family? Maybe you're part of that kind of church right now. We'll learn this week how Paul and his friends loved the church in Thessalonica—just like family.

PRAYER FOCUS FOR THIS WEEK

THE QUESTION: What is the writer saying?
THE ANSWER: How can I apply this to my life?

SUNDAY • 1 Thessalonians 1:1-5

DIGGING DEEPER Isn't it nice to hear someone say "thank you?" We all welcome people's appreciation for something we've done. God values our expressions of thanks as well. We should give thanks for even routine things such as meals, family members, and learning opportunities. When was the last time you thanked God for your church? Paul, Silas, and Timothy sent this letter together to the church they started in Thessalonica to let them know how thankful they were for them and how often they prayed for them.

Who can you say "thank you" to today? When was the last time you thanked God for your church? Are there any little things you are taking for granted that you should be thanking God for today?

MONDAY • 1 Thessalonians 1:6-10

DIGGING DEEPER One of the main problems among Christians today is similar to that of the early church: Believers were being persecuted for their faith. The Christians in the church in Thessalonica are a good example of what Christians should look like. They kept an attitude of joy despite persecution (v. 6), they consistently lived the Christian life in their community (v. 7), they shared their faith in their city and beyond (v. 8), and they testified of how God had changed their lives (v. 9). This is a great model for us to follow as we serve God in our own local church.

The church is only as strong as we are. Think about your personal example—can you say you have an attitude of joy, are consistent in your community, share your faith, and are praising God?

TUESDAY • 1 Thessalonians 2:1-8

DIGGING DEEPER When is the last time you met someone you thought you couldn't trust? What changed your mind about them, if anything? Paul gives the Thessalonians some reasons he was the real thing. He had suffered (v. 2) as he shared the Gospel. He made it a point not to be deceitful (v. 3)—he was as honest as he could be about what people were getting. He aimed to please God (v. 4) not people. Paul's point was that his lifestyle and words were honest and truthful, and that was how the Thessalonians knew he was from God and therefore trustworthy.

We can do a lot of flashy things to spread the Gospel, but what people want to know is that we really believe what we're preaching. What does your lifestyle say about you? Do people think you're honest?

WEDNESDAY • 1 Thessalonians 2:9-13

DIGGING DEEPER Imagine for a minute that you were called to a witness stand and challenged by a prosecutor to vouch for your best friend's spiritual life. Could you defend that person? Would it be difficult for you to honestly compliment his spiritual life or would you have to plead the Fifth Amendment and not say anything at all? When it comes to the Christian life it's important that what we say is backed up by how we live. The saying and doing should be the same. Paul and his companions are so confident in their testimony that they called the whole church in Thessalonica as witnesses to the fact that they were genuine. What they saw is what they got. **Could your friends vouch for your Christian life? Why or why not? What should you be doing about this today?**

THURSDAY • 1 Thessalonians 2:14-20

DIGGING DEEPER Have you ever really missed someone? Are there some people you love so much that nothing compares to being around them? Paul felt the same way about the church in Thessalonica. He saw them as family and had a "*great desire*" to see them in person (v. 17). Notice that there were people working very hard to keep them from seeing each other. This is a tool Satan has tried to use all throughout church history—he knows that if he can separate Christians, it will be easier to take us out. That's one reason New Testament writers encourage us often to pursue good Christian relationships. **Can you think of some practical ways you've seen the importance of other Christians in your life? Is there someone you need to make an effort to see today?**

FRIDAY • 1 Thessalonians 3:1-5

DIGGING DEEPER Christians aren't immune from trouble. We have problems just like everyone else. Paul says we are "appointed" for these problems (v. 3). A big New Testament theme—from Paul and others—is that God uses tough times to help us grow. One way He does this is as we are attacked by Satan or worldly influences, we get a better picture of Who God is. Another way this happens is that as God shapes our character, making us more like Him, we have to go through some pretty uncomfortable times. "Affliction" is to be expected (v. 4)—but so is seeing God work through it.

Think about the most recent tough time you've had. Can you see how God was working? How did you react? What can you do today to prepare for these times in the future?

SATURDAY • 1 Thessalonians 3:6-13

DIGGING DEEPER Paul was a great Christian already but look at what he's saying in these verses: He got the most encouragement from the example of the Thessalonians! Their testimony, growth, and the way they pursued Christ really comforted him (v. 7). Even though he was a very mature Christian, he still needed the encouragement of others to help him focus on God. The Thessalonians certainly weren't perfect—notice Paul's prayer requests for them in verses 9-13—but their commitment to growth was still encouraging.

No matter where we are in the Christian walk we can still be an encouragement to others by pursuing Christ. Who has encouraged you recently? Have you told them so or thanked them?

WEEK 48

As Paul finishes his letter to these growing believers he comments on an assortment of topics including holy living, the Rapture, relationships, and even the basics of Christian living. He has a lot for us to learn this week.

PRAYER FOCUS FOR THIS WEEK

THE QUESTION: What is the writer saying?

THE ANSWER: How can I apply this to my life?

SUNDAY • 1 Thessalonians 4:1-8

DIGGING DEEPER Have you ever wondered what the will of God is? Paul says God wants us to focus on one thing: holiness. It is part of Who He is, so as He draws us to Himself, He wants us to be holy too. The process where we move from our sinful nature to a holy new way of life is called sanctification (v. 3). In these verses Paul explains some ways to pursue sanctification and why it is so important. Sexual purity is important because it reflects the deepest relationships we can have on earth, which reflect how we connect with God. God wants us to treat others like we treat Him—with holy living (vv. 7-8).

Paul says the place to start with holiness is in our relationships. Why do you think this is important? Is there something in your personal life you need to change today?

MONDAY • 1 Thessalonians 4:9-12

DIGGING DEEPER What do you think most churches in America are known for today? Are they known for their buildings, size, problems, or even their pastors? Have you ever heard of a church that was known for its love? The church in Thessalonica had this reputation. In fact this church was so skilled at loving others Paul told them he didn't even need to address that area of their lives. They had already been taught of God to love one another (v. 9). Wouldn't it be great to be part of a church where people have loving relationships rather than fighting and squabbling over a lot of non-essentials?

What do you think most churches in America are known for? What are you doing in your church that will make it more like the church in Thessalonica? Where will you begin and whom will it involve?

TUESDAY • 1 Thessalonians 4:13-18

DIGGING DEEPER What happens to believers who die before Jesus comes back? This may not be an important question to you, but what if you were a new believer in Thessalonica and some of your loved ones had already died? Paul answers that question by saying that those who die before Jesus returns will not miss out but will instead experience the event in a different way. Paul says that "the dead in Christ shall rise first" (v. 16), meaning they're going to lead the way! Other believers will join them.

Do these verses give you comfort knowing what will happen? Are there other questions you are wondering about? Who can you go to for help with these today?

WEDNESDAY • 1 Thessalonians 5:1-8

DIGGING DEEPER Have you ever played a game of tag in the dark? It's easy to trip over rocks when you're running around. But imagine going around a corner to where a light is and suddenly being able to see everything. You can avoid the rocks now! That's what it's like for Christians. Paul says we are children of light (v. 5), meaning we can see what God has ahead. The unsaved, however, are in for a surprise. The "day of the Lord" is a time in the future when God will judge the wicked. Paul describes this time as a "thief in the night"—it will catch people off-guard, except for Christians who have been warned.

If you knew a friend was running toward a hole, would you try to give him some light? What can you do to share God's truth with unsaved friends today?

THURSDAY • 1 Thessalonians 5:9-15

DIGGING DEEPER Paul gives some very practical advice for how to make a church work well. These are not random instructions but are firmly rooted in verses 9-11 which say that we do all this because Christ died and gave us new life. He patched up our relationship with Him and is calling us to work on our relationships with others. This includes comforting each other (v. 11), encouraging people—especially those in authority (v. 12), and generally not stirring up trouble (v. 13). He gives more specifics in verses 14-15—all coming from a God Who already treats us the way He's asking us to act.

Do you obey the Bible because you know you need to or do you realize in your heart that these instructions reflect how God is already treating us? Which of these instructions needs your attention today?

FRIDAY • 1 Thessalonians 5:16-22

DIGGING DEEPER Paul gives us a tall order of instructions today, but remember—it's not a list of things to do; it's a reflection of how God is changing us! As we realize what Christ did for us at salvation and see how the Holy Spirit is working in our lives, we will see these attitudes and lifestyles becoming part of our behavior. Rejoicing (v. 16) isn't being a sociable person or always happy—it's an attitude of joy that comes from having the peace of God. Prayer (v. 17) or being in constant communication with God comes as we know Him more. Thankfulness (v. 18) is a result of seeing Him work. Other tips for staying on track include avoiding evil (v. 22), seeking out good (v. 21), listening to instruction (v. 20), and not pushing away conviction from God (v. 19).
Which of these areas would you like to see God improve in your life?

SATURDAY • 1 Thessalonians 5:23-28

DIGGING DEEPER Paul finishes his explanation of the sanctification process here. Look at Who is doing the work (v. 23)—it's not us! God is the One Who sanctifies. He can take people who are dirty with sin and decay and make us "blameless"—unable to be accused of a sinful lifestyle. In verse 24 Paul points to God's faithfulness. He's saying, "God wouldn't ask you for all this if He wasn't going to take care of it for you. He *will* do it." Do you ever feel overwhelmed in the Christian life? Do you feel like God is asking you to do a lot of hard—or impossible—things? **What can you do today to shift your focus? Do you need help from another believer to help you see how God, and not yourself, will do the sanctification work in you?**

WEEK 49

It's always great to hear from old friends. They can bring such rich encouragement. This week Paul again writes to his friends in Thessalonica and instructs and encourages them. As we read this letter may we be just as blessed and encouraged as they were.

PRAYER FOCUS FOR THIS WEEK

THE QUESTION: What is the writer saying?
THE ANSWER: How can I apply this to my life?

SUNDAY • 2 Thessalonians 1:1-5

DIGGING DEEPER Have you ever felt like saying "thank you" to someone who followed Jesus so closely it made a difference in your life? Paul did. In fact Paul commends not just one believer but the entire church of Thessalonica! The believers were growing in their relationships with God (vertically) as evidenced by their faith (v. 3) and they were growing in their relationships with others (horizontally) as evidenced by their love (v. 3). On top of that they were doing it in the face of persecution! No wonder Paul is so proud of them.
Who has been a great example of Christ in your life? Have you thanked them or encouraged them recently?

MONDAY • 2 Thessalonians 1:6-12

DIGGING DEEPER What do you think of when you hear "everlasting destruction?" Probably not warm fuzzy kittens—and you shouldn't because verse 9 says that phrase describes Hell itself. It is a place reserved for those who don't know God and never really wanted to know Him. Paul is setting up a contrast between the believers' lifestyle and that of the world. Those who worship themselves and follow their desires are doomed to an eternity of self and all the destruction that sin brings. Christians on the other hand are looking toward future glorification (v. 10)— an eternity of God, goodness, and all that He brings.

We often think of Hell as an arbitrary flame-filled place but Paul teaches that it's directly connected to our lifestyle. Do your choices point to the glory of God or yourself? Are you preparing for eternity?

TUESDAY • 2 Thessalonians 2:1-5

DIGGING DEEPER Paul is talking here about the end times where instead of the status quo we see now, God will pull back and let the earth be filled with wickedness (v. 3) until He intervenes again. The old sin nature will be given free reign for awhile. Paul says not to worry about this time (v. 2)—it's part of God's plan. After a "falling away" from God the Antichrist ("man of sin") will come to lead the rebellion. He will call for worship and the world which will no longer be restrained by the Holy Spirit will gladly and sinfully give it to him.

If you think the world is bad now realize that God is still involved and leading people back to Him. Who do you need to talk to today while you still have a chance?

DIGGING DEEPER Have you ever played with puppets? When you use a puppet you determine what it says and does. You control its personality, its voice, and its mannerisms—everything. You control it completely. The Antichrist, whom we see once again in our verses today, is nothing but a puppet. He is controlled by Satan himself. Satan is the real mastermind behind all the chaos, confusion, and conflict in the evil in this world. His ultimate goal is to ruin as many lives as he can and get as many people following him as possible.

How can you see Satan being a puppet master in the world today? What can you do to thwart his efforts? How will you start?

DIGGING DEEPER How are you feeling right now? Exhausted? Upset? Lonely? However you're feeling, be encouraged. God loves you. He cares about you. He has your best interests in mind. Let Him comfort your heart (v. 17). This sounds great—we know God is supposed to help us—but what does that actually look like? If you've never experienced it, see what Paul says in verses 13-16. He calls us to reflect on what God has done, look forward to what He will do, and follow the instructions of how He's called us to live.

Do you feel discouraged often? How much are the Christian disciplines— praising God, studying His Word, and praying—part of your life? God asks us to do these things because He knows it will help us focus on Him and He can give us real comfort.

FRIDAY • 2 Thessalonians 3:1-5

DIGGING DEEPER God is faithful. That statement may seem overused but for many of us there aren't a whole lot of things that we can count on. Friends have let us down, family members have disappointed us, and even church members have not been there when we needed them. To be fair we've let people down ourselves, too. But God has never let anyone down. When He says He will do something, we can count on it happening. In verse 3 Paul reiterates that God will not only "stablish" the believers (give them strength as He does His work) but will also protect them from temptation.
Does knowing God is doing the work give you confidence (v. 4)? Are you patient as God changes you (v. 5)?

SATURDAY • 2 Thessalonians 3:6-18

DIGGING DEEPER Do you ever go to church wondering what people will do for you? After spending time talking about the grand scheme of Christian living Paul gets down to some details. He encourages the believers to not take advantage of each other. All of them need to do some work. They shouldn't be "busybodies," gossiping and wasting time. If anyone does violate these rules, he should be treated with firmness but still love (v. 15). Notice Paul's directions in verse 13: Don't ever get tired of doing what's right.
Are you ever tempted to not work hard because others aren't? What does Paul say about this? Do you ever get caught up in being a "busybody?"

WEEK 50

Are you looking for the ultimate self-help book? Paul gives us some deep concepts this week to go with the simple truths we've always heard about God. Pay attention as Paul covers why we were created, what the point of life is, and where people can find real hope and fulfillment.

PRAYER FOCUS FOR THIS WEEK

THE QUESTION: What is the writer saying?

THE ANSWER: How can I apply this to my life?

SUNDAY • Colossians 1:1-8

DIGGING DEEPER Paul addresses this letter to the "saints." When Christ saves and forgives us we become *saints* positionally, even if we don't act like it in everyday life. Paul was thankful for these believers. They had a testimony of faith and love (v. 4) as they lived each day looking toward their future hope in Heaven (v. 5). These characteristics are what should set apart Christians today too—our trust toward God, our love toward each other, and a perspective that is always looking toward the fulfillment of God's promises: Heaven.

How are you doing in these areas? Is your life ruled by trust in God? How is your love toward others? Is your daily perspective looking toward Heaven?

MONDAY • Colossians 1:9-14

DIGGING DEEPER Do you ever look at all of God's instructions in the Bible and wonder where you should start? Paul's prayer request for the Colossians (v. 9) is also a great step-by-step instruction for how to live the Christian life. Notice that it doesn't start with doing good things; Paul wants us to begin with spiritual wisdom (v. 9). Once we have a better idea of Who God is, and He starts turning this knowledge of Him into results we can see in our lives ("wisdom"), the works and "walking worthy" (v. 10) will follow! Once we start living correctly, the process begins again with more knowledge. God gives us strength, patience, and joy as we grow (v. 11). **Do you ever get overwhelmed by all the instructions in the Bible? Do you struggle with being joyful and wise and patient and walking worthy of God? What do today's verses say about this? What are you responsible for?**

TUESDAY • Colossians 1:15-19

DIGGING DEEPER Paul's topic for today is nothing less than the point of life. Look at verse 16—*all* things, from the lowest plant to the mightiest spirit, to all the laws of nature were created for God. What does that mean? The world teaches us that living is about who can survive, who is the strongest or best, and where we can find fulfillment. God says living is about figuring out where we fit with Him. With sin altering the original setup, our focus now turns to Jesus Christ the "firstborn" (No. 1 in position and authority). He is the greatest example of creation working for God's glory. This is what makes Christianity different—we were created for a specific purpose and we have a Savior Who is God (v. 15). He shows us how to live. **Take a few minutes and think about what it really means when God says "You were created for Me." How does this affect your goals or ambitions?**

WEDNESDAY • Colossians 1:20-23

DIGGING DEEPER What does hope really look like? We know that salvation is great because we get to go to Heaven, but do we really know why Christ's work is so important and why hope is so great? Verse 21 says that in sin we were "alienated" from God—totally against Him with our minds not only wicked but also unaware how wrong we were. Christ not only brought all of creation back to Him undoing the disaster that sin caused but He took it a step further. We are now "unblameable" and "unreprovable." He's taken us completely to the opposite of where we were stranded with sin. We don't have to stay sinful. We can change.

We can often take Christ's work for granted because we're used to seeing the great results—hope and salvation. Have you ever asked God to help you really see your sin and how far you were from Him?

THURSDAY • Colossians 1:24-29

DIGGING DEEPER Do you like a good mystery? That's what Paul gives us today. God had been planning for years to send Christ and make things right in the world but the Jews only got to see some of the clues. They didn't know how it ended. Christ's death and resurrection and the arrival of the Holy Spirit wrapped together all the clues God had been giving people for years. Paul's job now was to spread the word letting people know what God had done (v. 29).

Mysteries are nice for those of us who get to see the end but not everyone knows the answer. Do you need to explain God's work of reunion to an unsaved friend today? Have you thanked God for solving the mystery in your life?

FRIDAY • Colossians 2:1-7

DIGGING DEEPER Have you ever seen someone struggle to solve a problem or try to build something without a good set of instructions? Paul's concern here is now that God has given us the answers, not all people are hearing them. That's why Paul encourages the Colossians to pursue understanding (v. 2) since he can't be there to share it with them in person (v. 1). He also warns about people who will be sharing false information (v. 3). Much of our roles as Christians today is getting the simple truth of the Gospel to people who are looking for answers.

How can you make sharing God's answers part of your everyday life? Who can you think of who needs some godly guidance today?

SATURDAY • Colossians 2:8-15

DIGGING DEEPER An important part of witnessing is understanding how we are made and why we live the way we do. Paul has already explained that we are created for God and can be reunited through Christ. Now he shows the different ways people try to find satisfaction. Our sin has made us incomplete—lacking—and people chase earthly love, fame, money, affirmation, or religion to try to fill that hole. They are looking for fulfillment and to feel like life has meaning. Even Christians do this—they look to God as a religion, figuring out their philosophy and doing good things (v. 8) but still missing something. Paul says only one thing takes us back to how we were created to be. One thing makes us complete (v. 10): Jesus Christ.

Are you ever frustrated with the Christian life? Do you feel like you can't live up to expectations? Where does God say your faults have gone (v. 14)?

WEEK 51

We get it, we get it! Jesus is supposed to be everything to us! But what does that look like? How should our lifestyles change to follow Christ? Paul gives us some very practical steps throughout this week. Let's see if we can live this out as we keep thinking about who we are in Christ.

PRAYER FOCUS FOR THIS WEEK

THE QUESTION: What is the writer saying?

THE ANSWER: How can I apply this to my life?

SUNDAY • Colossians 2:16-23

DIGGING DEEPER What makes other religions insufficient? We get the idea sometimes that we support Christianity like some people support a favorite sports team. But Paul says that it's a *lifestyle* difference. Look at verses 16 and 18. You may not have worshiped angels but have you ever become consumed with doing good things? Have Christian service or other activities become the focus of your spiritual life? They are part of being a Christian as Paul has showed us so far, but they are only important if they point to the real thing: Jesus. Do you want a shadow (v. 17) or imitation (v. 23) of what gives you life—or the actual source?

Look over verses 20-22 and try to think of some "ordinances" or "commandments" you've been told are important. Do you do these things looking at Christ or because they make you feel spiritual (v. 23)?

MONDAY • Colossians 3:1-7

DIGGING DEEPER What does it take to be a successful musician or sports star? Those people are all about practicing, right? We may even say that music or the sport is their "life." That's what Paul wants Christ to be for us (v. 4). Not only does Christ give us the power to live but He should also be the One we're focusing on. Paul is finally giving us the *how* here after spending two chapters telling us *why* Christ is everything to us. He says the key is to set our minds on things above. We need to think about Christ, want Christ, and make our desires Christ. The sinful things that grab at us are supposed to be dying (v. 5)—that's the life we *used* to have!
The move from death to life takes a while but it starts in our mind. Do you remind yourself that you are no longer stuck in your sinful desires? Do you try to focus your thoughts on Christ?

TUESDAY • Colossians 3:8-17

DIGGING DEEPER Paul is getting really practical in these verses. Remember in 1:9 when he said the growth process started with knowledge? He brings it up again here in verse 10. The key to putting on the "new man" is a better understanding of God, Who will then change us. In verses 5-9 Paul gives us specific examples so we can know what to get rid of in our lives. Verses 12-16 give us details of where we should grow. And verse 17 tells us how we do it—with all of our strength trusting in God's power.
Which of these characteristics stick out to you? How are you doing with knowing God—can you see Him working in you or are you still stuck on trying to do these things in your own power? Who can you ask for help with this today?

DIGGING DEEPER What do you think our society would look like if everyone followed today's verses? It sure would look different wouldn't it? There is something here for everyone. You may think the slave and master instructions do not apply today, but if you look at them like employees and employers, you can see that they do. Each of us is to work knowing that God is over us all. Verse 23 says God should be the reason we obey and verse 25 gives us an extra encouragement—God will take care of the people who don't live correctly.
Which of these categories do you fall into? Is there an area you should be looking to change? What can you do to remind yourself that it is God and not other people you are obeying?

THURSDAY • Colossians 4:2-6

DIGGING DEEPER When was the last time you seriously spent some time in prayer? Paul is telling us that prayer is the essential thing we need as believers to carry out the instructions he has given. Only through prayer for each other will we see lives changed and our service succeed. We are to pray with an attitude of thanks (v. 2) and for others to be able to share the Gospel clearly (vv. 3-4). Paul also reminds us of the importance of living a consistent godly life before unbelievers. We need to practice all of these parts of the Christian life to see them work together.
Which of these Christian disciplines needs more attention in your life: prayer, thankfulness, sharing the Gospel, or consistent living?

FRIDAY • Colossians 4:7-11

DIGGING DEEPER Paul points out some Christians who have really helped the work of Christ. Tychicus and Onesimus were taking this letter to the Colossians with instructions to tell them all about Paul and his ministry and to encourage them in the faith. Aristarchus was a fellow prisoner with Paul and had suffered much for the Gospel. Paul also mentions Mark, which is interesting because the two of them had a falling out earlier in their ministry (Acts 13:13; 15:37-38). Justus had also been an encouragement to Paul. God uses fellow believers to keep us all encouraged as we live the Christian life.

Who needs your encouragement today?

SATURDAY • Colossians 4:12-18

DIGGING DEEPER When you pray for people, what do you ask God for? Do you think about their spiritual needs? Verse 12 says Epaphras was praying that the Colossians would become perfect and complete—letting Christ do the work that Paul described in 2:10. In today's verses Paul also instructs the believers to share what he's written with other Christians (v. 16). We should not only be encouraging other Christians but also sharing what we've learned and how God has taught us to see Him better.

Can you think of some new prayer requests for the people on your prayer list? Who should you share with today about what God has been teaching you?

237

WEEK 52

Have you ever seen the total destruction from a fire or flood? It's not a pretty sight, is it? Joel predicts destructive consequences for those who refuse to repent. Have you ever wondered what the "last days" will be like? You'll get a good picture in the book of Joel this week.

PRAYER FOCUS FOR THIS WEEK

THE QUESTION: What is the writer saying?

THE ANSWER: How can I apply this to my life?

SUNDAY • Joel 1:1-10

DIGGING DEEPER Have you ever received a letter from someone you didn't know? What do you do? You probably look closely at it for clues. We can do the same with this book of prophecy. We know that Joel was a prophet whose name meant "Jehovah is God." He wrote around 835 B.C. He starts by telling us to share this message from God for generations to come. That would certainly include us today. He then describes the four major stages of the life cycle of the locust, an insect common in that culture. These words were being used as a warning to people of the devastation that was coming.

What do you do when you are warned about something? We're all familiar with God's warnings about salvation—can you pass this on today?

MONDAY • Joel 1:11-20

DIGGING DEEPER Have you ever wondered what it was like to live in Old Testament times? These people had an agricultural society with crops such as wheat, barley, grapes, figs, dates, and pomegranates. In today's passage all these crops were destroyed. The people were ashamed because the Law of Moses promised that God would bless their crops if they were obedient (Deuteronomy 28-30). Joel says that the disaster was a sure sign from God that all the people needed to repent. Their physical problems were just a sign of bigger issues.
Is God getting your attention with a hard time in your life? Are you more upset about how things have been messed up or are you concerned about making things right with God?

TUESDAY • Joel 2:1-11

DIGGING DEEPER Have you read a book or seen a movie that pictured a battle with endless numbers of soldiers storming a castle or battlefield? That is the picture Joel is giving of the coming destruction in "The Day of the Lord." This scene is describing the 722 B.C. destruction of the northern kingdom by Assyria, the 586 B.C. destruction of the southern kingdom by Babylon, and the A.D. 70 destruction of Jerusalem by the Romans. Joel sees this horrible day as a day of consuming flames, untold loss, and seemingly invincible foes. It is scary to fall into the hands of an angry, holy God. Our society tells us that God is love, which is true but He is also holy and just and must judge sin.
Is your life clean before a holy and just God? Do you need to confess sin to Him (1 John 1:9) and avoid possible destruction in your life?

WEDNESDAY • Joel 2:12-21

DIGGING DEEPER Have you ever lost hope in something or someone? An old saying goes, "While there is breath, there is life; and where there is life, there is hope." Joel is trying to get the people (and us) to see that there is always hope that they can repent and return to the God Who really loves them. To truly repent means a turning from or a changing of the heart and mind. It is agreeing with God that your previous attitude and behavior were wrong and that you need to change. It is being sorry and determining with your will to stop going your own way and to start going God's way.
Are there any attitudes or behavior patterns that you need to repent of?

THURSDAY • Joel 2:22-32

DIGGING DEEPER What do you need in life? No, not new music or video games. If you lived in Joel's time your basic needs would still be shelter and food. The reference to sitting under the vine and fig tree was talking about resting with plenty of their best foods out of the heat. Israel had been devastated but if these people would repent according to Joel's preaching they would experience physical blessings again. Verse 28 looks forward to the spiritual blessing that will accompany this revival. It is interesting to note that Peter quotes this passage in Acts 2 after the baptism of the Holy Spirit.
It's easy to get distracted by physical needs but God has promised to take care of these things once we focus on Him. Do you need to repent of anything?

FRIDAY • Joel 3:1-13

DIGGING DEEPER   Notice the universal scope of this section. "All nations" will be summoned to the valley of Jehoshaphat which means "Jehovah judges." It is another name for the Kidron Valley which runs north to south between the eastern wall of Jerusalem and the Mount of Olives. All three of the major monotheistic faiths (Judaism, Christianity, and Islam) refer to this valley to the east of Jerusalem as the place of the final judgment. We can read all about it in the book of Revelation. Now that you know where everything is going to end, what are you going to do with your life to be prepared for it?

When you're ready for the end you can make wise decisions as to what to do today. What do you need to do to be ready for the final judgment?

SATURDAY • Joel 3:14-21

DIGGING DEEPER   By comparing Scripture with Scripture (Zechariah 14; Isaiah 63; Joel 3; Acts 1; and Revelation 19) we can piece together this scenario of the return of Christ to establish His kingdom: Christ returns in the sky over the valley of Armageddon and speaks the destruction of the armies of the world. He touches down on the planet at the same spot from where He left—the Mount of Olives. He then pursues the attackers of His people down to Bozrah in the territory of Edom where He will crush them. Cosmic signs are associated with the return of Christ in Matthew 24 and Revelation 6. God will have the whole world's attention and there will be no doubt that God is helping Israel.

Spend some time comparing the Scriptures above to see for yourself what God has laid out for the end times. Are you ready?

The following chart is provided to enable everyone using Word of Life Quiet Times to stay on the same passages. This list also aligns with the daily radio broadcasts.

WEEK 1	AUG 28 - SEP 3	PSALMS 120:1-126:6
WEEK 2	SEP 4 - SEP 10	PSALMS 127:1-134:3
WEEK 3	SEP 11 - SEP 17	PSALMS 135:1-139:12
WEEK 4	SEP 18 - SEP 24	PSALMS 139:13-145:9
WEEK 5	SEP 25 - OCT 1	PSALMS 145:10-150:6
WEEK 6	OCT 2 - OCT 8	1 TIMOTHY 1:1-4:8
WEEK 7	OCT 9 - OCT 15	1 TIMOTHY 4:9-6:21
WEEK 8	OCT 16 - OCT 22	PROVERBS 26:1-28:28
WEEK 9	OCT 23 - OCT 29	PROVERBS 29:1-31:31
WEEK 10	OCT 30 - NOV 5	GALATIANS 1:1-3:9
WEEK 11	NOV 6 - NOV 12	GALATIANS 3:10-5:1
WEEK 12	NOV 13 - NOV 19	GALATIANS 5:2-6:18
WEEK 13	NOV 20 - NOV 26	DANIEL 1:1-2:49
WEEK 14	NOV 27 - DEC 3	DANIEL 3:1-5:16
WEEK 15	DEC 4 - DEC 10	DANIEL 5:17-8:27
WEEK 16	DEC 11 - DEC 17	DANIEL 9:1-12:13
WEEK 17	DEC 18 - DEC 24	2 PETER 1:1-2:22
WEEK 18	DEC 25 - DEC 31	2 PETER 3:1-JUDE 25
WEEK 19	JAN 1 - JAN 7	JEREMIAH 1:1-5:31
WEEK 20	JAN 8 - JAN 14	JEREMIAH 6:10-10:23
WEEK 21	JAN 15 - JAN 21	JEREMIAH 12:1-20:18
WEEK 22	JAN 22 - JAN 28	JEREMIAH 21:1-27:15
WEEK 23	JAN 29 - FEB 4	JEREMIAH 28:1-32:27
WEEK 24	FEB 5 - FEB 11	JEREMIAH 32:28-50:20

WEEK 25	FEB 12 - FEB 18	ACTS 1:1-3:11
WEEK 26	FEB 19 - FEB 25	ACTS 3:12-5:32
WEEK 27	FEB 26 - MAR 3	ACTS 5:33-8:13
WEEK 28	MAR 4 - MAR 10	ACTS 8:14-10:8
WEEK 29	MAR 11 - MAR 17	ACTS 10:9-12:25
WEEK 30	MAR 18 - MAR 24	ACTS 13:1-15:12
WEEK 31	MAR 25 - MAR 31	ACTS 15:13-17:21
WEEK 32	APR 1 - APR 7	ACTS 17:22-20:12
WEEK 33	APR 8 - APR 14	ACTS 20:13-22:30
WEEK 34	APR 15 - APR 21	ACTS 23:1-25:27
WEEK 35	APR 22 - APR 28	ACTS 26:1-28:31
WEEK 36	APR 29 - MAY 5	HAB. 1:1-ZEPH. 3:20
WEEK 37	MAY 6 - MAY 12	DEUTERONOMY 1:1-4:40
WEEK 38	MAY 13 - MAY 19	DEUTERONOMY 5:1-9:12
WEEK 39	MAY 20 - MAY 26	DEUTERONOMY 9:13-16:17
WEEK 40	MAY 27 - JUNE 2	DEUTERONOMY 18:9-34:12
WEEK 41	JUN 3 - JUN 9	JOB 1:1-10:22
WEEK 42	JUN 10- JUN 16	JOB 12:1-23:12
WEEK 43	JUN 17 - JUN 23	JOB 26:1-42:17
WEEK 44	JUN 24 - JUN 30	1 JOHN 1:1-2:27
WEEK 45	JUL 1 - JUL 7	1 JOHN 2:28-4:21
WEEK 46	JUL 8 - JUL 14	1 JOHN 5:1-3 JOHN 14
WEEK 47	JUL 15 - JUL 21	1 THESSALONIANS 1:1-3:13
WEEK 48	JUL 22 - JUL 28	1 THESSALONIANS 4:1-5:28
WEEK 49	JUL 29- AUG 4	2 THESSALONIANS 1:1-3:18
WEEK 50	AUG 5 - AUG 11	COLOSSIANS 1:1-2:15
WEEK 51	AUG 12 - AUG 18	COLOSSIANS 2:16-4:18
WEEK 52	AUG 19 - AUG 25	JOEL 1:1-3:21